Lucid Dreaming,
Waking Life

Lucid Dreaming, Waking Life

Unlocking the Power of Your Sleep

ELLIOT RILEY

Toplight

Jefferson, North Carolina

ISBN (print) 978-1-4766-8182-5
ISBN (ebook) 978-1-4766-4026-6

LIBRARY OF CONGRESS CATALOGUING-IN-PUBLICATION DATA
BRITISH LIBRARY CATALOGUING DATA ARE AVAILABLE

Library of Congress Control Number 2020020597

Front cover images © 2020 Shutterstock

Printed in the United States of America

Toplight is an imprint of McFarland & Company, Inc., Publishers

*Box 611, Jefferson, North Carolina 28640
www.toplightbooks.com*

Table of Contents

Table of Contents

Preface

$\mathcal{A}$ lucid dream is a dream in which you know that you are dreaming. I will define the term in great detail throughout this book, but that is the foundational definition.

I have had thousands of lucid dreams over the course of two decades. I began my journey with lucid dreaming around the age of eight. Even as a young child, I loved to ask people whether or not they had ever had a dream in which they knew they were dreaming. I found that, although people did not often discuss this phenomenon, most people I spoke to had in fact had this experience at least once.

For me, these dreams in which I knew I was dreaming were the closest I ever got to experiencing true magic. In these dreams, I had infinite power. I could fly. I could move objects with my mind. I could go anywhere in the world and do anything I pleased. I did not have to feel any fear, because nothing around me was real. I could make the dream be whatever I wanted it to be because it stemmed from my own imagination.

It was many years, however, before I came across the term "lucid dreaming." Once I knew that this hobby of mine had a name, and I learned that in fact people have studied lucid dreaming for centuries, I couldn't wait to read every book on the topic.

After reading the first book I could find on lucid dreaming, I started keeping a dream journal. I have continued to do so ever since. Over the course of nine years of dream journaling, I expanded my lucid dreaming practice through the guidance of trusted authors and researchers. I conducted my own lucid dreaming experiments, taking diligent notes about my experiences.

In college, I taught a lucid dreaming course to homeschooled students at an alternative learning center in Massachusetts. I couldn't wait to connect teens to this topic, since much of my avid exploration had taken off in my teenage years. As a lucid dreaming teacher, I grew familiar with the most common roadblocks that plague beginners as they learn to lucid dream. This book will provide techniques for overcoming those common hurdles, as well as the lesser-known challenges that can arise while cultivating this skill.

As a spontaneous, natural lucid dreamer, I had my first lucid dreams without actively trying to do so. That said, I still had plenty to learn. Over these two decades of lucid dreaming, I greatly improved the frequency and quality of my lucid dreams. Lucidity exists on a spectrum. Some lucid dreams are more logical, vivid, and malleable than others. I have honed my ability to have highly lucid dreams. Most importantly, practicing the skills involved in lucid dreaming has made me a calmer and more content person in my waking life.

This book will provide you with everything you need to know in order to begin having lucid dreams for the first time, or to improve the frequency, control, and clarity of your existing practice. I use the word "practice" because it is an accurate term to use. This word highlights the fact that lucid dreaming is a skillset, which you can learn, and improve, through dedicated effort. There is no one secret trick, no magic pill, herb, device, or app to ensure that you will have a lucid dream tonight, although this book will cover both ancient and modern tools for lucid dream induction.

I will provide fodder for the exploration of your dreams from a primarily psychological and scientific standpoint, and, to a lesser extent, explore various philosophical and spiritual perspectives on the topic. I offer advice on how to best take advantage of lucidity not just during your dreams; I also provide advice on leveraging your newfound skill for greater clarity during your waking life. What you gain from such a journey is yet to be determined. Lucid dreaming opens up a world of possibilities for self-improvement. All the tools you need are here.

SECTION ONE

How to Lucid Dream

It may seem unusual to start with an explanation of *how* to lucid dream, followed by an explanation of *why* lucid dreaming is worthwhile. I begin this book with a step-by-step explanation of how to lucid dream because I know from experience that you may be eager to get started experiencing lucid dreams for yourself.

Another reason for organizing topics in this manner is that the benefits of lucid dreaming are best understood through experience and are best applied once a foundational understanding of how to lucid dream has been established. Thus, while I will weave the benefits of lucid dreaming throughout this book, Section One will provide you with the tools you need to get started with learning how to lucid dream right away. Section Two will elaborate further on the benefits of lucid dreaming, offering suggestions for how to leverage your lucid dreams for greater personal insight, creativity, problem solving, and emotional regulation in your waking life. Finally, Section Three will cover recent findings in sleep science, as well as the more ancient insights of philosophy and spirituality.

Lucid dreaming offers people the chance to harness an underutilized part of their lives—sleep—for many of the same pursuits of their waking lives: greater happiness, clarity, and understanding of self. Thus, Section One will enable you to take greater advantage of the third of your life you spend sleeping, without further delay.

1

Definitions and Misconceptions

*H*ow do we use the word "dream" in everyday life? Phrases such as "the woman (or man) of my dreams," "my dream job," and "in your dreams" strongly associate dreams with the fulfillment of wishes, a perspective popularized by Sigmund Freud. The fact that people often recommend sleeping on your problems implies an intuitive understanding of the connection between sleep, problem solving, and emotional regulation.

After a difficult, emotional day, or a day full of problems to be solved, often the best thing to do is to sleep and return to those problems after resting your body and dreaming. Rest resets our emotions, and dreams provide a space to creatively approach difficult quandaries. The saying "life is but a dream" harkens back to ancient philosophical ideas about reality, which, as you will learn later in this book, some people take literally.

Thus, dreams have significance to our lives, and they can represent our greatest wishes as well as our greatest fears. We intuitively comprehend their psychological importance. Becoming aware that you are dreaming while the dream is still unfolding will open you up to a greater understanding of the dream state and thus will provide you with a greater understanding of yourself.

That is how people generally talk about dreams in everyday life in American culture. How do we discuss *lucid* dreams? Although the topic is gaining popularity, most people don't talk about lucid dreaming at all. Since the subject rarely makes its way into formal educational settings such as schools, there is a great deal of misinformation about lucid dreaming. When people do discuss lucid dreaming, much of their knowledge tends to come from media in the form of movies and television shows, or from individuals who have posted their experiences online. The creators of such content do not necessarily hold themselves to a high standard of accuracy. The primary goal of shows and movies is to entertain audiences. Such entertainment may lead to inaccurate or, at the very least, incomplete explanations of lucid dreaming. Individuals posting online may have educational rather than entertainment goals, but they tend to speak from their own experience alone. Such information is not always applicable to everyone. In this book, I will always indicate when my claims stem from my own personal experience alone, in which case, what I have concluded may or may not ultimately apply to your lucid dreaming journey. For that reason, I have also incorporated a good deal of scientific research, from which you can draw broader generalizations.

As stated earlier, a lucid dream is a dream in which the dreamer is aware that she is dreaming. At its core, lucid dreaming is a simple concept, and yet this topic is plagued with confusion. While the bare-bones definition of lucid dreaming is straightforward, many people struggle to understand it.

In my formal and informal experience as a lucid dreaming teacher, one of the most common questions I am asked is "Was *this* a lucid dream?" Clearly, a significant number of people struggle to understand what does and does not qualify as a lucid dream.

Lucid dreams have a reputation for being vivid and easy to control. These factors can be true, but not necessarily. A good deal of variation exists in terms of the content of lucid dreams. Think about all of the variation that exists in the psyches of individuals: remember that we carry these psyches to the dream state. Our minds build our dreams, and minds differ quite a lot from one another. At every opportunity, I aim to provide a neurodiverse perspective on lucid dreaming.

The most important thing for you to remember about the definition of the term "lucid dream," is that knowing you are dreaming while in a dream is the one and only defining feature of a lucid dream. Some people note that their lucid dreams are particularly vivid. On the one hand, it is possible to take advantage of your lucidity in order to make a dream more vivid. Since you understand that you are dreaming, you can consciously try to heighten your senses. This is an enjoyable and grounding activity for the start of your lucid dream, and a useful technique to utilize if you notice that the dream is fading.

Some people claim that their lucid dreams are *inherently* more vivid than their non-lucid dreams. While I am not saying that this is impossible, I want to point out another plausible explanation, which is that perhaps lucidity prompts these dreamers to notice or realize, for the very first time, how vivid and realistic dreams *are*.

Both lucid and non-lucid dreams can be vivid. Either type of dream can also be dull. The intensity of the sensory elements of your dreams is affected by several factors. Awareness that you are dreaming *may* be *one* of these factors, but it is by no means the only factor. How long you experience your current sleep phase is another such factor. If you are in REM (rapid eye movement) sleep for a considerable amount of time and then soon transition to another sleep phase, the visual elements of your dream may start to fade by virtue of this fact alone, making the dream less vivid.

Two years ago I had a very frustrating lucid dream. I fully understood that I was dreaming and had confidence in my ability to influence my visual surroundings. Nevertheless, I couldn't see much of anything. Everything was extremely bright and washed out, which not only frustrated me, but hurt my eyes. Luckily, since I knew I was dreaming, I was not in fear for my eyesight. I tried to improve the visual elements of the dream, a technique I had successfully used in past lucid dreams, but my effort had no impact. Upon waking, I realized that the curtains of my hotel room were wide open. The sun had been shining directly onto my shut eyelids, rendering it impossible for me to see.

In this case, I had a lucid dream which, due to external factors, was not at all vivid. Had I not been lucid, the dream would have had the same dull visual atmosphere. This is an example of a rare case, but it serves to demonstrate that vividness is a factor irrespective of lucidity. It may seem that I'm nitpicking, but if you wish to learn about lucid dreaming then you must begin with a solid foundational understanding of the definition of a lucid dream. If you don't fully understand what a lucid dream is and what it isn't, you are much less likely to have one and to recognize it when you do. I am highly invested in understanding how dreams work and relaying that information as accurately as possible to readers.

As I alluded to earlier, one potential explanation for lucid dreams' reputation for being vivid, is that perhaps people do not take note of vividness in their non-lucid dreams. You may wake up from a non-lucid dream amazed because of how real the dream felt to you, but in a lucid dream you are able to take note of the dream's detailed nature *while it is occurring*. One of the most amazing things about lucid dreaming is that it allows you to observe your dreams *as dreams* while they are occurring, and often your primary emotion will be awe at how utterly convincing the hallucination is.

People tend to be amazed that their dreams can be simultaneously vivid and convincing, yet unreal. I have experienced this phenomenon firsthand and I understand what this awe feels like. One thing that lucid dreams can serve to teach us is that reality is not determined by vividness of experience; reality is determined by a shared experience of external stimuli among two or more witnesses.

We all experience reality a little differently from one another. Anyone who has ever argued over whether an object is blue or purple knows that we don't all see the world the same way. We most certainly do not all categorize, analyze, or assess our experiences in the same way. But disagreeing over whether a shirt is blue or purple is different from seeing a purple shirt that no one else sees. The latter is a hallucination. (We could argue further whether shared hallucinations are possible, but that is a separate issue.)

I am not a particularly visual person, and I have difficulty imagining things in my mind's eye while awake. My favorite dream activity is observation. I often pick up a small object, such as a leaf, and marvel at the artistry of the details—details that I would not be able to conjure in my mind's eye while awake. It feels as if I know so much more than I consciously realize. My brain stores this information somewhere, somehow, even though I'm unable to access it while awake.

To review, lucid dreams need not be vivid. Non-lucid dreams can also be vivid. It is possible that lucid dreams feel more vivid simply because the dreamer is more likely to notice, consider, and remember the realistic nature of dreams while having the metacognitive experience of lucid dreaming.

Much like vividness, control is neither necessary nor sufficient for a dream to be considered lucid. Contrary to popular belief, dreamers often try and fail to exert control over their lucid dreams. For example, in a lucid dream you might attempt to turn a menacing figure into something harmless. This could work, but it might not. What's really useful about lucidity is that it allows you to problem solve with near-infinite creativity. Understanding that the external reality you're experiencing is neither external nor real allows you to deal with the experience effectively. You may decide to exert control in order to alter your perception; however, that is but one tool in your toolbox, and it is a tool which does not always work.

In later chapters I will discuss methods for dealing with nightmares, executing difficult tasks, and attempting other forms of control in a lucid dream. I will explain the factors that can affect your level of dream control. I will also discuss times when there are more effective methods at your disposal than attempting to exert control over your surroundings. For now, understand that you might not always be able to control everything about your lucid dreams.

What's more, you may be able to exert control over your non-lucid dreams. A friend recently relayed the following dream story to me: "I was at work and we were playing this gambling game. I was able to make the winning numbers appear. I didn't know I was dreaming, but I think it was a lucid dream. I was controlling things." I hope it is clear to you by this point that this was not a lucid dream. If you don't know you're dreaming, it is not a lucid dream. My friend's misunderstanding is part of the problem that arises when we conflate the definition of a lucid dream with secondary factors that may or may not be present within lucid dreaming, such as vividness and control. This example also demonstrates that control, like vividness, can be present in non-lucid as well as lucid dreams.

Control is often an element in my non-lucid dreams. While I don't know on a conscious level that I'm dreaming, perhaps I recognize on a subconscious level that I am able to conduct impossible tasks, such as flying away from enemies or changing the scenery. I do not attempt these feats while waking, so there must be some type of awareness of the added possibilities of the dream state, even though I do not consciously realize that I'm dreaming in this particular case. The more you solidify your understanding of the differences between your waking and dreaming mind states, the more likely it is that you will experience controlling a non-lucid dream.

Another plausible reason why people assume that all lucid dreams are vivid, or that all lucid dreams can be controlled, is that these are major selling points for lucid dreaming. If you tell people you are able to have dreams in which you know you're dreaming, you will be met with a range of positive and negative reactions, including interest, disinterest, jealousy, skepticism, and confusion. Some people may not initially understand what's so special about this kind of dream, but if you go on to explain that in lucid dreams it's often possible to control elements of the dream in various ways, such as changing the scenery, making people and objects appear and disappear, and more, those initially disinterested listeners may become intrigued.

It is easier to explain the fun of controlling your dreams, or engaging in activities such as flying or sex, than it is to explain the subtler joys of lucid dreaming. These subtler joys include the awe-inspiring wonder at simply looking around at a convincing illusion, a hallucination just as detailed as your waking perception, all the while knowing that what you see is a product of your own mind. That explanation is a mouthful, compared to saying "you can control lucid dreams."

My favorite thing about lucid dreaming has nothing to do with controlling the dream or seeking out pleasure in the dream realm. It is the moment when I realize I'm dreaming. Dreams typically involve conflict, which I will refer to in this book as "plot." In a dream, I am always striving toward something or running away from something, either physically, metaphorically, or both. These dream plots are often stressful and overlap with my most profound fears and concerns. For that reason, it is always a relief to discover, before waking, that the plot I'm wrapped up in isn't real.

Now that I have clarified the definition of a lucid dream, in the following chapter I will detail some of the amazing features of lucid dreams and explain why I think nearly everyone should strive to dream lucidly.

Why Learn to Lucid Dream?

This book is split into three sections: how to lucid dream, why to lucid dream, and sleep science and philosophy. The why section will go into detail about how you can use lucidity to deal with nightmares as well as waking anxiety, what kinds of uses lucid dreaming offers for your waking life, the many purposes of dream analysis, lucid dreaming's connection to creativity and meditation, and more. This chapter briefly explains some of those whys, with the purpose of increasing your motivation to put in the work of learning this skill.

Perhaps the most compelling reason to learn to lucid dream is in order to take full advantage of the time you have at your disposal. I can only speak from an American perspective, but everyone in my life is pressed for time and wishes they had more of it. While the majority of Americans do not sleep enough, people generally sleep for approximately one-third of their lives. If you are the type of person who mourns this time spent sleeping as a waste, getting better acquainted with your dreams can help transform your view on the matter.

In this book, you will also learn about the vital physiological role of sleep. Sometimes, I feel reluctant to go to bed on a weeknight, knowing that I will wake up and have to go to work. It feels like no time will pass in between, but that isn't true. In these instances, I remind myself that during those eight hours, I will be doing the important and enjoyable work of sleeping and that if I pay attention, I may have a lucid dream or at least wake up with the memory of interesting, non-lucid dreams.

The alluring possibility of lucid dreaming may help you to better prioritize sleep, if you are not already doing so. Sleep is essential for emotional regulation, memory, and problem solving. Getting a healthy night's sleep is the first step towards lucid dreaming. I assure you that this first step will also greatly improve your mental and physical well-being. As you become increasingly conscious of the experience of falling asleep, you will discover that there is much enjoyment not only in lucid dreaming, but also in exploring other sleep phases more intentionally than you have in the past. Hypnagogic imagery, the geometric visual hallucinations that accompany the transition from wakefulness to sleep, provides a beautiful and interesting experience if you take the time to notice it. Certain induction techniques for lucid dreaming will ask you to do just that.

Another initial reason for learning how to lucid dream is to increase your dream recall. This process will get you more acquainted with the world of your dreams. Dreams are far too undervalued in modern Western society. Dreams can simply be interesting or entertaining or funny, but they can also assist you in achieving a deeper understanding of yourself and your mind. Even if you are not easily able to lucid dream right away, increasing your dream recall and analyzing your dreams through dream journaling will provide you with psychological insights.

I previously mentioned that one of sleep's functions is to improve problem-solving skills. Lucid dreaming can help you to harness the full potential of sleep as a realm for tackling difficult problems in your life, whether those problems are personal or theoretical. Through the skill of lucid dreaming, you can take your quandaries to the dream world and work on them there.

Creative pursuits, such as writing, art, and music, can also be explored in the dream state. I have used lucid dreams to write music, which I would never have been able to write while awake. You can create art in a dream that you simply could not make in your waking life, and while you cannot take it back with you physically, you can gather inspiration from dreams and utilize that bank of inspiration while awake. If you don't consider yourself an artist, creative pursuits may simply be intriguing activities for you to try in a lucid dream. Grab a paintbrush and paint directly on the sky!

Similarly, you can practice other skills within a dream, not just creative ones. Coaches and music instructors often ask their athletes or students to visualize a game or performance. Lucid dreaming takes this one step further by providing a virtual reality space in which you can feel like you really are running track, playing soccer, or dancing in a ballet. Make the most of your time by practicing in your sleep. You can even rehearse speeches and presentations, increasing your confidence through practice.

If you are a religious or spiritual person, lucid dreaming may have added significance for you. You might consider this state as a time for you to pray, meditate, or ask spiritual questions. Even if you are not a spiritual person, posing a question aloud in the dream world can produce interesting and surprising "responses" for you to consider upon waking.

Similarly, some lucid dreamers like to use the dream state to attempt to improve physical ailments through meditation or other means. I am not a medical professional and cannot fully endorse this as a means of healing, but it does not appear that it could do any harm, especially in conjunction with medical care.

Lucid dreams can be a space to heal old psychological wounds as well. They provide the opportunity for you to rehearse a difficult conversation with a loved one, or to have a conversation you could not possibly have in waking reality. You can attempt to find closure with people who are no longer in your life.

I highly recommend consulting a therapist to assist you with this kind of exploration, so that you have someone to talk to if this brings up buried emotions. In future chapters, I provide guidance on conducting these experiments. In the next two sections, "Who Should Learn to Lucid Dream?" and "Cautions and Caveats," I discuss the difficulties you could potentially encounter while lucid dreaming. I will help you to decide if this practice is really the right thing for you to engage in at this time.

Who Should Learn to Lucid Dream?

Who should learn to lucid dream? In short, *nearly* everyone. Whether your primary goals in life are creative, pleasure-seeking, spiritual, or health-focused, there is something for you to discover and improve upon through this practice. However, I must put my passion for the topic aside and realize that lucid dreaming isn't for everyone. I will illustrate this through two examples.

In the first example, my college roommate, a dear friend of mine, had spontaneous lucid dreams occasionally and without effort. I encouraged her to try new things in her lucid dreams or to have lucid dreams more often, but she simply had no interest. She said that her dreams felt like video games, and were fun, but the fun was lost when she realized that she was dreaming and no longer knew what to do. While I find this difficult to relate to, I'm not in the business of proselytizing. Just like meditation, prayer, the arts, and even exercise, lucid dreaming is simply not for everyone.

That said, there is virtually no risk that someone who picks up this book does not have any interest in lucid dreaming. Thus, I can leave this example aside. However, sometimes, someone can have an interest in lucid dreaming but would be better off not exploring it. I know this from direct experience with a different friend of mine, which serves as my second example. I lent this friend my copy of *Exploring the World of Lucid Dreaming* by Stephen LaBerge. Visiting his house months later, I noticed that his bookmark was still in the first chapter, and I chided him for not reading faster. He explained that, following LaBerge's advice, he had begun asking himself whether or not he was dreaming periodically throughout the day.

My friend had a history of mental health issues, including depression and trauma. For most people, lucid dreaming can help with these issues. However, my friend also struggled with psychosis and had considerable difficulty understanding his own mental states. When he asked himself whether or not he was dreaming, unlike the vast majority of people who do so, he genuinely could not tell whether or not he was dreaming. He started to feel like perhaps he *was* dreaming, and this uncertainty plagued him until he put the book, and the question, out of his mind. Essentially, trying to lucid dream had caused a break from reality for him. This experience was temporary and ceased once he stopped reading the book and stopped attempting to lucid dream, but nevertheless the book did cause him temporary harm.

Prior to these two friendships and discussions, I had advocated for everyone to explore lucid dreaming. I now know that this was short-sighted of me and, unfortunately, led in one case to real harm. For that reason I want to warn any readers who struggle with psychosis, schizophrenia, or similar diagnoses to proceed with caution. I am not necessarily saying that they avoid lucid dreaming completely; that choice is up to them. I only have one example I can offer of someone with psychotic tendencies practicing lucid dreaming, and in his case, it caused him temporary distress. Only you can decide whether exploring this topic is right for you. If you are seeing a therapist, I highly recommend discussing the matter with him or her.

Psychologist, psychotherapist and Webster University professor Brigitte Holzinger argues for similar restraint when she writes, "My concern is that patients with psychosis or leaning toward a loss of a sense of reality may not be suitable candidates for lucid dreaming."[1] She does not argue that certain individuals should unequivocally avoid lucid dreaming, but rather she recommends that patients with psychosis, histrionic tendencies, and/or narcissistic personality disorders proceed with caution, if at all, in learning to lucid dream. She further recommends that they do so while under the careful guidance of a therapist.

Even if you do not experience breaks from reality, you may be concerned about the impact that lucid dreaming could have on the quality of sleep you're getting. Since lucid dreaming is a more logical state than non-lucid dreaming, might it cause you to feel less rested upon waking? Authors Ursula Voss and Georg Voss note that "it takes effort to dream lucidly" and that their research participants reported that "such dreams are easily interrupted by noise or state of mind." While you might experience more awakenings as a result of practicing lucid dreaming, it is unlikely to significantly impact your overall sleep quality because it is unlikely that *all* or even most of your dreams will be lucid.

Some induction techniques ask you to rearrange your sleep schedule using alarms that are meant to wake you during REM sleep, which could, of course, impact your overall sleep efficiency for that night. That said, these techniques are not necessary to learn to lucid dream, and if you are interested in trying them, you could make a choice to do so only on a night when you are able to sleep late the following morning.

In fact, learning to lucid dream could potentially improve the amount of sleep you get, if you become inspired enough by the prospect of these dreams to increase the amount of time you spend in bed. This book will also touch on some basic tips for dealing with insomnia and sleep problems. If anything, you should leave the experience of reading this book with at least the same quality of sleep that you currently experience.

Something to consider when you evaluate whether or not this practice is for you is that you are unlikely to have lucid dreams every single night unless you make a serious and concerted effort to do so. This book will give you the tools you need in order to have and to explore lucid dreams. While the book will hopefully open a doorway for you to enter a new mind state, lucid dreams are rare, and putting down this book and ceasing your efforts to have lucid dreams will result in much fewer occurrences of them.

It takes effort to sustain lucidity. Even if you realize you are dreaming, certain effort is necessary to not forget this information over the course of the dream. Thus, if you have a lucid dream essentially against your will, you have the option to dismiss this information and continue engaging with the dream plot. In short, while I can lead you through a doorway, you are welcome to turn back and leave at any time.

Cautions and Caveats

There are two more caveats before I start connecting you with tips for learning how to lucid dream. They are the related topics of sleep paralysis and lucid nightmares.

Sleep Paralysis

Most of the complex and memorable dreams you have occur during the sleep phase of REM. REM is named for its characteristic rapid eye movements, but REM has many physiological symptoms besides that. REM sleep is also characterized by fast, low amplitude and desynchronized brainwaves, which are similar to the brainwave patterns we have while we're awake. For that reason, REM sleep is sometimes referred to as "paradoxical sleep." Unlike when we are awake, we are unconscious of our surroundings in REM. In REM, our amygdala, which plays a central role in memory, decision making, and emotional response, is 30 percent more active than it is when we're awake. Finally, REM sleep is characterized by muscle atonia, a nearly complete paralysis of the body.

While paralysis of the body sounds frightening, and indeed it can be, it is entirely necessary. In fact, the inability of a body to effectively paralyze itself during sleep is a chronic condition known as REM behavior disorder. It is debilitating and quite dangerous if untreated. Muscle atonia prevents us from moving our real bodies in order to act out our dreams.

Sleep paralysis, therefore, is a natural and necessary aspect of sleep. When people use the term "sleep paralysis," however, they are generally not referring simply to REM-induced muscle atonia, but to a state in which the sleeper is aware of her own body's paralysis. Sleep paralysis occurs when we are either falling asleep or waking up.

In my own personal experience, sleep paralysis is more likely to occur in the morning when I've had significant sleep, in other words eight or more hours, and in particular it is likely to occur during a night of interrupted sleep. If I awake during REM, for example, and remain awake for half an hour or more, I tend to have sleep paralysis when I return to sleep.

Part of the good news is that waking during REM, staying awake for half an hour, and going back to sleep is also a method of inducing lucid dreams! The braver among us may even want to view sleep paralysis as something to seek out, as it provides a direct path to lucidity.

Sleep paralysis is relatively common.[2] Therefore, you will probably have experienced it before. If you have, knowing about its essentially harmless nature and its connection to lucid dreaming can potentially help you to better handle any distress from the experience. For those of you who have not experienced sleep paralysis, I include this information among the caveats, because learning to lucid dream can cause you to experience sleep paralysis for the first time or cause you to have an increased incidence of sleep paralysis.

To review, an increase in sleep paralysis experiences is not exactly a physiological phenomenon. Your body is always paralyzed during REM sleep. You are simply not usually aware of this fact. Certain lucid dreaming techniques which I will discuss in this book (namely wake-induced lucid dreams) require the dreamer to remain consciously aware as she is falling asleep. Studying the transition from wakefulness to dreaming may cause you to become aware of your body's paralysis. Again, I encourage you in this instance to remember that sleep paralysis is not dangerous and is in fact essential in keeping you safe from harm.

What's more, once you have entered sleep paralysis, you are on the brink of a dream, potentially a lucid one. Whether you are experiencing sleep paralysis as you fall asleep, or as you are waking up, you have the ability from this state to relax and fall back into a dream. Sleep paralysis can sometimes be accompanied by hallucinations; however, you are more conscious of your true external surroundings during sleep paralysis than you are during a dream.

In sleep paralysis, you can feel your real body in bed, and you are generally aware of where you are physically. This is an ideal state from which to enter a lucid dream because your mind is thinking relatively clearly. Since you are not yet in a dream, you also can influence the content of your dream before it even begins. You can decide, for example, that you'd like to dream about being on a beach, so you imagine the sights and sounds of a beautiful beach landscape. Soon it will appear before you, and you will no longer have the fear of sleep paralysis, because you will be able to move your *dream* body. In sleep paralysis, in general, try to focus on moving your dream body rather than your physical body.

Only you can decide whether the risk of experiencing sleep paralysis outweighs the possibility of experiencing the joy of lucid dreams. I recommend that you view sleep paralysis as the natural, healthy occurrence that it is, and that you also see it as an opportunity to transition directly to a pleasant lucid dream. You do not have to follow my advice, of course. Most people react to sleep paralysis by trying desperately to move. This effort often takes several minutes but usually does result in waking up and being mobile again (if not, you may slip into a dream). People who frequently experience sleep paralysis develop their own methods of dealing with it, which often include focusing on moving one small part of the body, such as a finger, until achieving mobility in other areas.

One of the major problems with this technique is that as soon as you successfully wake up and move your body, what then? You will likely want to go back to sleep, but now you are afraid to do so. Once you have experienced one bout of sleep paralysis, it is possible to end up in a cycle of several bouts of paralysis in a row. While it can be satisfying to move, and while it temporarily relieves fear, your fear will return when you realize that you have to make a choice between losing sleep by remaining awake, or going back to sleep only to have another paralysis experience. What's more, moving your dream body and entering the dream state relieves fear just as effectively, and it brings with it the benefit of a lucid dream.

If you end up having several bouts of sleep paralysis in a row, remind yourself that you have the option to fall back asleep from the paralyzed state and then embody your dream self. While you may feel frightfully restricted in sleep paralysis, remember that the endless possibilities of the dream world are at your disposal.

In general, though, paying attention to the dream state in a concerted and mindful way can simply make you more aware than you have previously been of the fact that when you're dreaming, you are not in control of your real body, which can be quite scary and concerning. For example, I have had dreams wherein I was incredibly thirsty but no amount of water could satiate my thirst. This led me to realize I was dreaming, but all I wanted was to wake up and drink water.

In another dream, I could hear my actual alarm going off but for some reason the alarm would not wake me. Here are my notes from that experience:

> *I have sleep paralysis. I decide to take advantage of the opportunity so I get up out of bed with my dream body. I know that my first alarm has already gone off and another will soon. I do some exploring in the area outside of my dorm. Soon, my alarm goes off. I can hear the real alarm in the dream. I can't wake up or move my real body. I want to turn the alarm off and feel bad about it continuing to play on a loop while my roommate might still be trying to sleep. I dream that my roommate comes over to my bed to turn the alarm off. Upon waking, she confirms that the alarm did go off and she was wondering why it wasn't waking me. She did not really turn the alarm off in real life—it must have eventually stopped and I dreamt up an explanation for this.*

In sleep paralysis, breathing can be restricted, and someone might hallucinate that a figure is resting on his chest. With decent control of breathing, however, you can use your breath to calm yourself. All that said, you will not necessarily experience sleep paralysis just because you are trying to lucid dream. I cannot say for certain what role, if any, sleep paralysis will play in your lucid dreaming journey.

Lucid Nightmares

In addition, if you dedicate yourself to this practice and ultimately end up having frequent lucid dreams, it is rather likely that you will experience the often-overlooked phenomenon of a lucid nightmare. It is my hypothesis that if you already suffer from frequent nightmares, you are at a higher risk of having a lucid nightmare than someone whose dreams tend to be more neutral or positive.

In addition to the assumption that all lucid dreams can be controlled, people also can assume that lucidity dissipates all fear. It certainly can, and that is one of the major uses of lucidity, but matters are not always that simple and straightforward.

The way I tend to explain lucid nightmares is by comparing them to anxiety. If you have ever felt anxious, you know that the emotions of fear and stress can overtake you, even when you fully understand that what you are worried about may never come to pass. If you have experienced clinical levels of anxiety, then you know that the physiological and emotional effects of anxiety (feelings of distress, pounding heart, sweating, digestive problems, difficulty thinking) can come out of nowhere.

If, in that moment, someone were to tell you that you need not worry because your concerns are not "real," this information would have little impact. You might already know that you are experiencing a bout of anxiety or even a panic attack. The first time that you have a panic attack is usually the most frightening, because you might believe that it is a medical issue, such as a heart attack. The knowledge that what you are experiencing is in fact anxiety can prevent you from making an unnecessary trip to the hospital, but the physiological and emotional symptoms will not simply disappear because you know they are "not real."

If you have never experienced this clinical level of anxiety, then simply think of a time when you were severely distressed about something which you were almost certain would not actually come to pass. Perhaps, out of almost nowhere, you start to worry that your family member who did not return a call or a text got into a car crash and is now dead. While you know it isn't likely, and you understand that your own mind is the sole source of this fear, you may not be able to relax until you have proof that your loved one is okay. You may be able to think of nothing else until you hear from this person. It is the strength of the emotion, not the logic behind it, that takes over and prevents you from being able to do or think about anything else in that moment.

Similarly, in a nightmare, even if you become lucid and you know that the menacing features of the dream are not real, you might not be able to relax until you wake up. In a lucid nightmare you may want to wake up as a means of escaping the emotion itself as well as the unpleasant perceptions of the dream. Remember that the amygdala is 30 percent more active in REM than it is when you're awake, making these emotional experiences particularly strong.

In a dream, much like in the case of anxiety, sometimes the feeling of fear actually precedes the presence of fearful imagery or ideas. In dreams, our expectations determine our reality. With your amygdala in overdrive, you may suddenly feel worried, anxious, or frightened. After the emotion arises, your dream will respond by providing you with something to blame for the emotion.

Here's an example. I had a lucid nightmare once, wherein I was in my house and the phone rang. I didn't know who was calling. Out of nowhere, I suddenly felt scared. The thought occurred to me that maybe I shouldn't answer the phone, because what if someone dangerous was on the other line? I answered the phone and immediately *knew* (as is so often the case in dreams) that the person on the other end wanted to kill me. The emotion of fear preceded a mental explanation, which led to a dream event. In waking life, we tend to assume that our emotions are logical reactions to external stimuli, but they can arise without a clear explanation. When asleep, our dreams tend to provide an explanation for the emotions we are experiencing.

Just like in the waking example of worrying that your friend has been in a car crash when you know it is most likely untrue, in dreams it can be very difficult to let go of your fight-or-flight reaction, even when you know that everything you are perceiving is a hallucination. The physiological experience of fear courses through you, and in turn, your mind responds with images and sensations of your deepest anxieties. These "unreal" experiences can be *even more frightening* than real-life fight-or-flight scenarios. Also, contrary to popular belief, it is possible to experience physical pain in a dream.[3] This pain might result from something occurring within your real body, or it can be psychosomatic. Either way, dream pain feels the same as waking pain. Who are we to say that it isn't "real" or that it need not be feared?

So, in fact, becoming lucid can actually turn an otherwise neutral dream into a nightmare. In my personal experience, this understudied phenomenon is much less common than the experience of lucidity that leads to feelings of joy and elation, but it can happen. If you have had any life-threatening, traumatic experiences in your waking life, you might notice that certain everyday sensory inputs can trigger feelings of anxiety when you are reminded of the traumatic experience. For example, I was in a car crash on the highway in the rain. Now, whenever I am driving on the highway in the rain, I feel nervous and viscerally remember the trauma I experienced years ago. I can even smell the smoke and burning rubber. Consider then the possibility that the dream world itself, especially for those who have actively explored the dream world at length and experienced numerous nightmares, can serve to trigger similarly nerve-wracking feelings. The dream world, though we call it a "world," is not a place. It can feel like a place, but it is a state of mind.

If you realize that you're dreaming, then you are also realizing that you are in a place where terrible, frightening things have happened to you, so it is not surprising to think that the lucid realization could change the tone of the dream to become more negative. The dream world itself can be a traumatic trigger for frequent nightmare sufferers. Lucidity is the realization that you are in the dream world; thus, lucidity itself can change a dream into a nightmare.

To review, becoming lucid does not immediately dispel all fear in all cases, and becoming lucid can in fact evoke fear in an otherwise neutral dream. That said, those are initial reactions to lucidity. With practice and guidance, you can absolutely use lucid dreaming as a means to deal effectively with nightmares and turn them into positive experiences. I want readers to fully understand how lucidity operates and to be able to make informed decisions before getting started with that process. All of that said, I fully believe that you would be better off psychologically with the tool of lucidity than you would be without it.

Even, and in fact especially, if you experience frequent nightmares, lucidity can cure them, but it is more akin to therapy than to a pill. It takes time, practice, and your own active involvement, but if you learn how to lucid dream, you will influence your dreams and move them in a positive direction. Understand, though, that this may not be an entirely linear process and that lucid nightmares could occur.

For now, be aware of both the good and the bad, the joyous and the frightening, that lies ahead if you pursue lucid dreaming. Nightmares are a part of life, regardless of whether or not you learn to lucid dream, and in fact lucid dreaming will help you to deal with nightmares. But first you need to learn effective ways of leveraging lucidity against your fears. It is not always like turning on a switch.

If you have read this chapter and remain interested in pursuing lucid dreaming, please proceed to the following chapters, in which I will provide concrete tips for achieving lucidity often and with ease.

2

Tips to Get Started

*I*n American culture, the allure of lucid dreaming has led to the emergence of individual gurus, courses, drugs, and technologies, all promising you the ability to lucid dream—*tonight!* They argue that, by having these instantaneous, effort-free, lucid dreams, you will be able to *control* your dreams and *control* your life. This is a far cry from more ancient lucid dreaming practices in other cultures, such as the Tibetan practice of sleep and dream yoga.

In our busy, individualistic culture, we want results fast. We want to purchase self-improvement, peace of mind, or enlightenment, but these things cannot be purchased, no matter how much money you spend. What's more, you do not need to spend money to attain greater understanding and peace in your life. Information is the only thing you need in order to learn to lucid dream, and that information can come from an inexpensive book, a free website or video series (as long as it's trustworthy!) or a knowledgeable friend. There is no one path for learning to lucid dream, but I assure you that the path does not need to cost much financially.

People want to learn to lucid dream without any effort, and they want to use lucid dreaming to control their dreams. It is my view that the *effort* it takes to learn to lucid dream is worthwhile in and of itself. By trying the exercises and meditations in this book, you will become better acquainted with the inner workings of your own psyche. You will learn to pause in moments of daily stress to ensure that you are awake and not merely dreaming these stressors. You will become more aware of the present moment.

There is effort involved in learning to lucid dream—just like there is effort in learning any new, worthwhile skill. It is a joyful effort. Quick-fix gurus and tech manufacturers who promise you the gift of lucid dreaming without the effort are actually robbing you of greater understanding of yourself, greater recognition of your dreaming mindstate, and greater levels of present-moment awareness and calm in your waking life. My approach does not promise you control of your dreams, but I do promise you greater control over yourself, your emotions and your reactions to stimuli. I promise you greater control of yourself in both waking and dreaming, rather than a fleeting control within one or two particular dreams.

At this point, ideally you know the definition of a lucid dream, you understand the beneficial possibilities of having a lucid dream, and you are unconcerned by my cautionary tales about occasional frightening aspects of this practice. You understand that learning to lucid dream takes effort, and that the effort is pleasurable and worthwhile in and of itself. Great! How do you get started?

The chapters "Increasing Dream Recall," "Reality Checks," and "Induction Techniques" will each go into great detail about the main ways you can work towards becoming lucid. Before going into such detail, I want to provide a short introduction to each of these topics. My reason for sequencing matters in this way comes from my experience as a young lucid dreamer. Authors understandably want to begin with an in-depth definition of important terms as well as with some historical, cultural, or scientific context. Often, like me, they want to provide you with reasons to learn to lucid dream as well as some cautionary information, all at the outset.

Then, those authors go into detail about each step of the lucid dreaming process. It can be frustrating to read through those beginning chapters and give each step of the process its due attention when you just want to get started *right now*. Thus, in this chapter I provide a condensed list of advice, so that you can start a lucid dreaming practice today. Each step is covered in detail in later chapters.

The first step towards becoming lucid is to increase your dream recall. The reasoning for this is that, for one, if you have a lucid dream but you don't even remember it, what use is it to you? Furthermore, understanding the general content of your dreams will help you to recognize them as they are unfolding, thus helping you to become lucid more often.

One effective way to increase your dream recall is by keeping a daily dream journal. This step is highly integral to your practice. Unfortunately, for a lot of people interested in learning how to lucid dream, keeping a dream journal is the most difficult hurdle to overcome. Don't worry about how you are going to sustain a dream journaling practice over the long term. Focus on making sure you write down the next dream that you remember, whether that is after a nap today or after you wake up tomorrow morning.

Today, solidify your intention to remember your dreams and write them down by saying or thinking, *I will remember my dreams.* Tomorrow morning, the first thing you think about when you wake up should be your dreams from the previous night. You may want to use a visual signal, such as a sticky note on your nightstand, or a note accompanying a phone alarm, to remind you to think about your dreams as soon as you wake up. When you arrive at the section about keeping a dream journal, I will give you all the tips I know to make dream journaling an easy habit for you to maintain over the long term.

The second step, performing reality checks, is something you can do *right now.* Take a moment to sincerely ask yourself whether or not you are dreaming. Don't dismiss the question; really think about it. Try to do this as often as possible today.

The third step is learning how to induce a lucid dream. One method that you can easily try tonight is called autosuggestion. Before going to bed, choose one of the following phrases to say to yourself (in your head or out loud), *I will have a lucid dream. I will be aware that I am dreaming.*

My personal favorite autosuggestion phrase is *The next thing I see will be a dream.* This phrase needs to be said or thought with eyes closed in order for it to be true. With your eyes closed, you may see some wisps of light and color known as hypnagogic imagery. At that point, you are not yet immersed in a dream. Remind yourself that whatever you see *next* will not be real. It will be a dream. If you have visual difficulties, you can modify this technique by saying, *Whatever I hear/feel next will be a dream.* Try to sincerely expect yourself to recognize your perceptions as a dream when they arise. Confidence is key.

Now you have a handful of techniques you can try right now, later today, and tomorrow morning, in order to work towards having a lucid dream. Each of these tips deserves further exploration, consideration, and practice in order to be most effective. The following chapters will provide that context for you.

It Starts During the Day

Lucid dreaming is a skill that is ultimately practiced and cultivated in sleep. However, the role of waking consciousness in having lucid dreams cannot be overemphasized. Ultimately, lucid dreaming is a practice of increasing awareness throughout your waking and dreaming life. As Tenzin Wangyal Rinpoche points out in *The Tibetan Yogas of Dream and Sleep*: "If we are too distracted to penetrate the fantasies and delusions of the moving mind during the day, we will most likely be bound by the same limitations in dream." Achieving a lucid dream begins with the act of *stopping* the external actions of your body and ceasing the thought stream in your mind, in order to assess the reality of your situation before proceeding any further with your thoughts and actions.

Focus on performing reality checks during your waking life. Eventually, if you practice often enough during the day, you will naturally begin practicing reality checks during sleep. Lucid dreaming practice involves taking a metacognitive look at your waking thoughts and perceptions. Rinpoche goes on to explain this by reminding his readers that "the 'you' that lives the dream of waking life is the same 'you' that lives the dream of sleeping life. If you spend the day spaced out and caught up in the elaborations of the conceptual mind, you are likely to do the same in [a] dream."[1]

In contrast, if you spend the day in awareness, on the lookout for incongruities that are characteristic of dreams, you are more likely to spot them in a dream. Take stock of your greatest fears, desires, and recurring thoughts during the day, as those are what you are most likely to dream about tonight, in one form or another.

Similarly, if you simply take note of your mind's impact on external reality during waking life, you are more likely to become aware of its impact in a dream and become lucid as a result. In dreams, the impact of the mind on seemingly "external," perceptual reality is undeniable. All of your dream perceptions are created by your mind. Practitioners of sleep and dream yoga argue that waking life functions in exactly the same way. You do not have to go so far as to call dreams and reality "the same" in order to recognize the impact of the mind in both states. While external reality is not, as far as I can tell, *created* by the mind in the same way that dreams are, the mind still creates much of what we take away from external reality in the form of meaning.

Consider simply the impact that your mood has on your day. If something happens that you perceive and label as a bad thing, it can upset you. Carrying your upset mood with you throughout the day can have a real impact on your perceptual reality. Feeling the emotion of anger, for example, makes it all too easy to find additional external events to be angry about. You may be more likely to treat someone with disrespect, leading to a tiff or a full-blown fight, leading in turn to more anger. Thus your anger serves as a self-fulfilling prophecy and has a tangible impact on external reality. This is not to say you are not entitled to feel angry. It is perfectly natural, healthy, and normal to feel negative emotions such as anger. I am merely using this as an example to illustrate how the mind impacts external reality in subtle but undeniable ways. The more you practice metacognitive activities such as lucid dreaming or meditation, the greater you will be able to understand this connection and hopefully disrupt it.

To give another example, consider the importance expectations have on your waking reality. Throughout this book, I will argue that dreams directly follow the mind's expectations, and I urge you to hone your expectations for the results you wish to bring forth. In the waking world, your expectations do not have such a direct, demonstrable, and immediate effect as they do in the dream world. Your fear of your house being broken into does not lead immediately to a stranger jimmying the lock on your front door. That said, your expectation to have a terrible day may very well cause one. In contrast, your expectation that your job interview will go well can cause it to go well. A fear of failure can be enough to ensure failure.

The visualization and autosuggestion techniques described in this book can help you in your waking life, beyond simply providing a means of lucid dreaming more frequently. I will provide one example from my own life. One night I was bowling with some friends of mine. I go bowling at most twice a year; it is by no means a hobby of mine. I tend to avoid participation in most games and sports in general, as they make me feel self-conscious. In spite of my self-consciousness, though, I can be exceedingly competitive. Thus I found myself in the ridiculous position of wanting to be good at something that I have no reason to be good at.

In any case, I found myself reciting a strange mantra during this bowling game. Whenever it was my turn, I would say to myself, *This is a dream. I'm dreaming.* I tried to have the same kind of influence over my environment that I have in a lucid dream. In other words, I tried to completely *expect* a strike. I visualized myself knocking all the pins over. I bowled with the full expectation of this working. It was primarily a visual technique, rather than a physical one.

My bowling noticeably improved. The mental act of cultivating positive expectations and visualizing those expectations playing out had a stronger impact on my ability than any physical tweak I made to my bowling style. I have since practiced the technique of trying to exert a dreamlike control over my surroundings in various contexts. It has an undeniable impact, but likely this impact must be experienced to be believed. Try it. Try it in a bowling alley. Try it out before talking to someone you think is cute. Try it before a job interview. It can't hurt, and you have much to gain in understanding how your mind works.

Lucid dreaming is as much a waking life journey as it is a dream journey. Focus now on performing reality checks (asking yourself whether or not you are dreaming) and honing your expectations in your waking life. Try to exert a lucid-like attitude toward your waking life. There is a great deal of potential improvement to be gained through this practice alone, and lucidity in the dream state is likely to follow.

Organizing Your Goals

Learning to lucid dream is a process of creating and meeting personal goals—big and small, short term and long term. Throughout this book you will be asked to create and assess goals for yourself. Organizing your intentions can help you to stay focused throughout this process. It is a purely mental skill, and, often, would-be lucid dreamers have to self-motivate in the absence of formal classes or clear-cut rewards. There-

2. *Tips to Get Started*

fore, solidify the most important internal rewards you wish to gain, and stay focused on those. Don't give up. Remember that many of the steps required to become an avid lucid dreamer, such as keeping a dream journal or performing reality checks, are worthwhile in their own right.

Increasing your dream recall is enjoyable because in so doing, you will have more memories. You will no longer feel like sleep is a blank time wherein nothing happens to you. Keeping a dream journal allows you the opportunity to mine your psyche for hidden treasure in the form of self-understanding. Asking yourself whether or not you are dreaming is a meditative practice which helps you to stay grounded in the present moment. This kind of present-moment awareness is likely to quell your waking anxieties, regardless of whether or not this leads to a lucid dream right away.

You are welcome to chart your lucid dreaming goals in any way you wish. I will include a recommended schedule of goals and activities, which you are welcome to follow at your own pace. Keep in mind that trying to tackle too much too soon can lead to frustration and burnout; however, an absence of concrete goals can just as easily lead to giving up. Try to find a balance which works for you.

At this beginning phase, I recommend the following goals and activities:

Week One Goals

1. Keep a daily dream journal.
2. Perform at least one reality check per day.
3. Identify your most important reason for learning how to lucid dream. Write it in your dream journal, or somewhere where you will see it in the future. Return to this overarching goal whenever you feel your motivation slipping.

29

3

Increasing Dream Recall

*T*he first step towards lucid dreaming is to increase your dream recall. Everyone dreams, whether they realize it or not. People who claim that they "never dream" simply aren't remembering their dreams. This can happen for several reasons which I will discuss.

What can you do to increase your dream recall? First, if you are someone who struggles to remember dreams, do not get hung up on this fact. Remember the importance of outlook and expectation to the practice of lucid dreaming. If you say to yourself and to others, *I never remember my dreams*, this may become a self-fulfilling prophecy. Instead, even if it is true that you rarely remember your dreams, tell yourself that you will remember at least one of your dreams tonight. Setting an intention and an expectation to remember your dreams will help you to do so. Similarly, never say anything along the lines of *I can't lucid dream*. Even if you have been trying to dream lucidly and have not yet succeeded, do not set yourself up for failure through this line of thinking. Believe in your ability to remember your dreams and to dream lucidly.

It may be worthwhile to keep in mind that considerable variation exists in dream recall from person to person. In his study of 193 college students, David Watson tracked the frequency of dream reports over a period of fourteen weeks. His findings demonstrate a remarkable range, including 11 participants who reported dreams less than 10 percent of the days and another 11 students who recalled dreams on more than 90 percent of the days. One participant reported no dreams at all, and two participants had dream recall rates of 98 percent. With an individual range of difference from zero to nearly 100 percent, this study provides reason to believe that there are natural differences in dream recall. What I recommend taking away from this is not to beat yourself up for starting this process with a low dream-recall rate.

These natural differences in our baseline tendency to remember our dreams may be due in part to personality. Watson found that high dream recall was positively correlated with openness to experience and unrelated to the other Big Five personality traits (conscientiousness, extraversion, agreeableness, and neuroticism). Watson found that "individuals who are prone to absorption, imagination, and fantasy" report more dreams than those who are less prone to such mental activities.[1] If you are someone who is open to new experiences, prone to fantasy, and has a high dream-recall rate, that's good news. If that does not describe you, though, don't worry. These innate differences in dream recall do not mean that you can't make a significant difference in your own dream recall through lifestyle choices and techniques.

For many people, the most important lifestyle choice you can make to increase your dream recall is to go to bed sober. There is no substitute for natural sleep. Alcohol consumption before bed can lead to frequent awakenings and a decrease in deep sleep. Therefore, consuming alcohol before bed not only makes it less likely for you to remember your dreams when you wake up, it also greatly decreases the overall quality of your sleep.

Marijuana has perhaps an even more detrimental impact on your likelihood of remembering your dreams. While many people appreciate that marijuana makes them sleepy and as a result can help them fall asleep, it also completely alters the makeup of sleep in ways you probably do not even realize. Marijuana consumption decreases the amount of REM sleep you have. As I previously mentioned, REM is the sleep phase in which most of your complex dreaming occurs. It is the sleep phase in which you are most likely to experience a lucid dream. Consumption of marijuana will make it much less likely for you to have a lucid dream because it will cause you to have fewer dreams overall.

There is a phenomenon known as REM rebound, which occurs when daily marijuana users cease their intake of the drug. Their REM sleep will not only return to normal levels but will actually surpass those levels, causing a detoxing user to have more dreams than someone who never smokes at all.[2] So for that reason, if you are currently using marijuana before bed, don't worry! If you stop tonight, you will have far more dreams than you normally do, even more dreams than the average person. You will be much more likely to remember your dreams, and to have a lucid dream, if you stop smoking marijuana altogether or at least cease consumption for several hours before sleep.

If you struggle with insomnia, I recommend that you see a doctor who will treat you holistically and not prescribe sleeping pills. Besides going to bed sober, one of the most important things you can do to get a good night's sleep is to avoid screen time, such as watching television, using computers, and looking at smartphones, before bed. The blue light from such screens suppresses the production of melatonin, a hormone that regulates the sleep-wake cycle.

In contrast, there are natural things you can do to help your circadian rhythms function properly and work to your advantage when trying to fall asleep. Taking a hot shower or bath is one of these activities. Doing so increases your body temperature temporarily. Then it leads to a dip in your core body temperature, which is also a feature of your natural circadian rhythm, thus it helps you to feel more tired. Similarly, keeping your bedroom around sixty-five degrees is ideal for sleeping. It may sound a little on the cold side, but, again, a dip in your core body temperature around bedtime will actually help you fall asleep.

Next, going to bed and waking up at the same time every day is one of the most powerful lifestyle changes you can make in order to help regulate your sleep. It can be difficult to avoid sleeping late on the weekends, but your body will thank you, and your lucid dreaming practice will improve. For more information on insomnia as well as the biological function of sleep, I recommend the excellent book *Why We Sleep* by Matthew Walker.

Another facet to increasing your dream recall involves changing your mental habits in the morning. Especially on workdays, most of us wake up and begin thinking about what we have to do. We mentally plan our outfits or our breakfasts. We immediately reach for our phones to start scrolling, or we hop straight out of bed to go shower or wake our kids.

If you really want to expand your consciousness into a greater understanding of yourself and your dreams, you need to rework your morning routine. This may sound complicated or difficult, but it doesn't have to be.

You don't have to take considerable time in the morning to contemplate and write down your dreams (though you can). You *do* need to create a new mental habit of immediately asking yourself upon waking what you were just dreaming about. This need only take a few minutes. You can spring out of bed or reach for the phone after you have taken the time to recall your dreams.

Immediately upon waking, try not to move or to open your eyes. If your alarm wakes you, turn it off, close your eyes and return to the position in which you were sleeping. Try to remember what you were dreaming about. With practice, you will find that you are much better able to recall your dreams if you make remembering them your first waking thought, than if you wait an hour or two until later in the morning. Closing your eyes and keeping still serves to keep your mind focused on this task.

There is something about lying in bed with your eyes closed that prompts your mind to think about and recall dreams. There have even been days where I could not remember my dreams at all until the following evening, but as soon as I lay my head down on the pillow, I remembered my dreams from the night before. The importance of keeping your body still, preferably in the position in which you were sleeping and with your eyes closed, cannot be overestimated.

Once you remember a dream or two, you need to record at least part of one of your dreams. You may feel like you will remember the dream later and you don't need to record it. After all, dreams are vivid, distinct, and full of meaning. But dream memories are not like waking memories. Even when you feel totally confident that you will remember it later, you probably will not remember the dream unless you write at least some of it down.

Keeping a Dream Journal

A dream journal is the most powerful tool at your disposal for increasing your dream recall. Going to bed sober and thinking about your dreams first thing when you awake will help you to remember your dreams, but you will lose these memories quickly if you don't write them down. Keeping a dream journal has two main purposes: one, to increase your dream recall, and two, to assist you in analyzing the content of your dreams.

As long as your system for keeping a dream journal allows you to achieve those two goals, it doesn't matter precisely how you do it. You can use a physical journal and pen, or an app on your phone. You can write about every dream you remember, or just one per night. You can track whatever information you find most relevant to your lucid dreaming practice. You can even voice-record your dreams if you see some advantage in doing so. If you do decide to use a physical dream journal, keeping it by your bed can help serve as a visual clue for you to think about your dreams both as you wake up in the morning and as you transition to sleep at night.

As a lucid dreaming teacher, I have often seen students abandon their lucid dreaming practice almost entirely at this step. I understand from personal experience how difficult it can be to form this new habit. I attempted to keep a dream journal for many years before I was able to make it a daily habit. That is why I want to leave the details open-ended and provide room for whatever personalization you need in order to sustain this new routine.

My love of sleep, which makes me such an avid dream explorer and lucid dreamer, is often the very thing that makes dream journaling difficult. I can't manage to exit the dream world and crawl out of bed early enough in the morning to provide adequate time for dream journaling on days when I have somewhere I need to be.

The way I worked around this difficulty was to split up my dream journaling into two parts. When I wake up in the morning, I make sure to stay as still as possible and to ask myself what I had been dreaming about. I wait until I feel that I've remembered as much as I can about the content of my dreams. Then, I open my eyes, and take out my phone. The main reason for using my phone is that it is simply quicker for me than writing by hand. A secondary reason for using a phone is that I tend to have my phone on me at all times, unlike my various notebooks, so I can ensure that I will have access to it throughout the day in case new dream memories pop up. Even if I am traveling and sleeping in a different place, I have my phone with me. Throughout the day whenever dream memories emerge, I write down a few sentences about them.

I do not write out every single detail at this first step. I make sure to write at least a sentence or two about the most pertinent aspects of my remembered dream or dreams. I have learned through experimentation that I have to write at least a sentence for it to spark my memory later. I have tried on occasion using just a few words or phrases—like "Ocean. Family." This is not enough for me to remember the dream.

Later on in the day, when I have a moment, I return to my notes on my phone and open my physical dream notebook. I date each entry, and write as many details as I can recall about my dreams. I make sure to note whether or not I experienced sleep paralysis, and I describe any and all lucid dreams. I circle the words "lucid" and "sleep paralysis" in the journal so that I am easily able to flip through and find these entries, in order to read through my recent lucid dreams and also to track how often I am having them. Tracking sleep paralysis allows me to see how it is connected to lucid dream frequency.

I'm a writer, and I'm not a very visual person. If you, on the other hand, are more visually inclined, you may wish to draw or diagram portions of your dreams along with your entries. My two-step process of note-taking in the morning, followed by writing a full journal entry later, has allowed me to easily maintain a daily dream journal habit for more than nine years. For that reason, I encourage you to do anything you need to in order to make this practice as straightforward and sustainable as possible.

If you are doubting whether your dream journaling practice is robust enough, return again to the goals of dream journaling. Is journaling helping to increase your dream recall? This is something you should be able to track. Is the number of dreams you remember each night increasing over time? If you can roughly estimate how many dreams you used to remember before keeping a dream journal, has that number increased?

Ask yourself additionally if the entries you've written are providing you with enough information to be able to analyze patterns in your dreams. You may want to return to this question later, in the section about dream analysis, when I outline the sort of information that is useful for inducing lucid dreams. For now, know that as long as you are meeting these two goals with your dream journaling, then your methods for doing so are working just fine. If, however, you don't have enough detailed entries to adequately analyze your dreams, you will want to expand your journaling.

I let myself off the hook when it came to writing entries first thing in the morning, once I discovered that this was not sustainable or entirely necessary for me. I also came to terms with the fact that I am not able to write an in-depth entry on every single dream. I follow my own dream-recall advice. As often as I can, I go to bed sober, I think about my dreams first thing in the morning, and I keep a dream journal. For this reason, I have excellent dream recall. I tend to remember several dreams each night. I simply do not have the time, then, to write an entry about each one. I make sure to write about at least one dream from each night, as long as I can remember one.

I always write detailed entries about my lucid dreams, even if I have more than one in a given night. I also write detailed entries on any dream that feels personally meaningful or relevant to my dream analysis practice. It is up to you how many dreams you write about each night, if you remember more than one. It should be a matter of which dreams you deem most important. Your dream journaling is also likely to morph over time as your lucid dreaming goals change.

Tracking Your Progress

Keeping a dream journal provides you with data to track your progress and to discern potentially useful patterns in your sleep behavior. I recommend numerically tracking your lucid dreams each month. I track my lucid dreams, as well as the number of nights I could not remember a single dream, and the number of times I experienced sleep paralysis. I do all of this on a monthly basis. At the end of each year I calculate my average number of lucid dreams per month and compare this figure to previous years.

Tracking my lucid dreams allows me to set goals for myself and to take note of whether I've met them. Over the years, I have tracked patterns such as which months of the year I tend to have the most or the least lucid dreams. If you are interested, you can also look at the days of the week when you are most likely to lucid dream and focus your effort on those days. You will likely have more lucid dreams during nights when you can sleep for eight or more hours.

The possibilities for data tracking are virtually endless. Keeping track of how many nights I am able to remember at least one dream, versus the nights I do not recall any dreams, gives me another important metric for measuring my success or failure. I highly recommend making a dream-recall goal *before* making a lucid dreaming goal. As I've already stated, improving your dream recall will make it more likely for you to have a lucid dream. Additionally, since this is a mental skill, it is important to avoid mental blocks against lucidity. Don't try to take on too much too soon or to make lofty goals you cannot achieve. Give yourself a pat on the back whenever possible. Lucid dreaming is a difficult skill to learn, and an undervalued skill at that. Thus, you are unlikely to receive a lot of positive, external reinforcement or support. Give yourself permission to celebrate seemingly small victories such as remembering a dream and writing it down. Many people give up at this initial stage.

The best way to set achievable goals is to set goals in relation to where you currently are. Thus, if you have never had a lucid dream in your life, setting a goal of having five per month would be too high. In fact, even one per month would be too high. Instead, first take the time to measure your current status. Commit to a month of dream journaling before anything else. This will be enough of a challenge.

At the end of that month, take note of whether or not you had any lucid dreams. You may also want to take note of whether or not you experienced sleep paralysis, either with a lucid dream or separately from one. Take note of whether you were able to harness sleep paralysis for lucidity or chose to wake yourself up instead. Tackling and taking advantage of sleep paralysis is a challenging long-term goal for many people.

If, at the end of the first month, you didn't have any lucid dreams, don't worry! Instead, focus on how many nights you were able to recall and record your dreams. If you were able to write only ten dream entries, for example, whether that was due to low dream recall or difficulty remembering, that is perfectly fine. Think of it this way: that's ten more dreams recorded than last month. Perhaps it's the first ten dreams you have ever written down. Take time to appreciate what you've done: you set a goal (keeping a dream journal for at least one month) and stuck to it.

Next, make a new goal, one which will challenge you but you know you can achieve. Someone who recorded ten dreams in her first month could strive for fifteen next month. You may very well surpass your initial goal. Just make sure you set one. If you happened to have a lucid dream in the first month of this process, you might want to make a goal to have two next month. That said, you might make just as much lucid dreaming progress by focusing instead on improving your dream recall and dream journaling habits. Those foundational skills will help you in the long run to build a dedicated practice around respecting and analyzing your dreams. This foundation of recall and journaling may even help you to become a true oneironaut (explorer of the dream state) more than the initial excitement of your first few lucid dreams will.

One of the main reasons to focus your initial goals around dream recall and dream recording is that your dream journal will provide you with a wealth of information to analyze. In addition to tracking the data I've already mentioned, you could take note of things like how much you slept each night, as well as your sleep schedule. If you have different alarm times on different days, you may want to keep track of that as well.

Research indicates a connection between meditation and lucid dreaming, as well as video-game play and lucid dreaming.[3] If you are a frequent meditator, you may want to track your meditation practice alongside your lucid dreaming to see if there are any patterns to be discovered there. Similarly, if you are an avid video-game player, you may want to track the hours you spend gaming, and cross-reference this with your dream data. Take the time to ask yourself if there is anything about your waking life which may be positively or negatively correlated with instances of dream recall, lucid dreaming, or both. We can all be citizen scientists in this under-researched field of study.

Analyzing Your Dream Content

Logical incongruities often alert us to the idea that we may be dreaming. These logical incongruities can be outlandish and impossible occurrences, such as a talking animal. They can also be a lot subtler and harder to detect. While there are overarching properties to dreams, and frequent categories of incongruity to look out for, individuals also differ considerably in terms of their dream content.

For me, one of the most common incongruities that alerts me to the fact that I'm dreaming is a matter of time and place. I dream that I am in college, or high school, or some other time period from my past. I almost always realize that I'm dreaming in these dreams, in part because I have had these types of dreams so many times in the past and used them to become lucid on countless occasions.

You probably have dreams of past stages in your life at least occasionally, but this may not turn out to be the most important incongruity in *your* dream world. Perhaps you are more likely to dream about a person from your past. Or perhaps it is more common for you to discover objects or animals behaving in strange and impossible ways.

These incongruities can be highly specific, due to our personalities and individual experiences. As a young child, I frequently had dreams in which I would see duplicates of my cat. I would see one of her, then turn a corner and see her again. I might enter a room and see more than a dozen copies of this cat. The first few times I had this dream, I was not lucid and felt very distressed by the image. After the second or third instance of this particular dream symbol, I was able to consistently use this incongruity to become lucid.

Note that this example constitutes a recurring dream. If you notice through this process of dream analysis that you have any recurring dreams, take special note of that in your dream journal. You should be able to use recurring dreams to become lucid fairly easily. Becoming lucid in a recurring dream may even be a way of gaining closure on this particular dream image or event that seems to be haunting you with its persistent appearance in your sleeping mind.

Given how personal these telltale dream images and events are, you will want to read through your dream journal and consciously look for your own incongruities. Stephen LaBerge called these incongruities "dreamsigns," and he identified four main categories of dreamsigns: inner awareness, action, form, and context.[4]

Inner awareness refers to our thoughts, emotions, sensations, and perceptions. I argue throughout this book that thoughts and emotions behave differently in dreams than they do in waking life. Emotions can appear out of nowhere and then result in the dreamer finding a source externally. Thoughts can similarly appear out of nowhere. While this is certainly also true in waking life, the form and impact of these random thoughts function very differently in the dream world. For example, in dreams, you may have sudden thoughts of entirely new information, such as *I've been fired from my job!* In the waking world, this is not how we gather information, but often in dreams we believe our own thought-data without questioning it, and these thoughts therefore drive our absurd dream plots.

If you pay careful attention in your dreams, you will be able to catch these thoughts as they arise, and then demand evidence for their claims or perform a reality check following the thought. Those are two areas of difference I have found between the dreaming and waking worlds, but I reiterate the individuality of this process. Perhaps you more frequently experience unusual sensations or perceptions than thoughts or emotions.

To provide a personal example of an action dreamsign, I have had countless dreams in which I have shoplifted. I never shoplift in real life. I have theorized as to why I dream about shoplifting even though I never wakefully shoplift, and concluded that even in non-lucid dreams I am often subconsciously aware that I'm dreaming and thus behave more impulsively and less ethically than I do in real life.

This theory applies to other dream behaviors of mine. In real life I am quite shy, but in dreams I often lean over and kiss the cute person next to me. If anger wells inside me in a dream (recall the added strength of dream emotions), I may yell at the top of my lungs. I am very unlikely to do that in real life. Can you identify any similar behaviors in your own dreams? They partly depend on your waking personality. I am less likely to notice characters or objects behaving strangely in my dreams, but perhaps those will be frequent action dreamsigns for some readers.

The dreamsign category of form refers to ego form, character form, setting form, and object form. You may have dreams in which you inhabit an entirely different body or perspective than you do in your waking reality. It is very common for characters and settings to blend together in dreams. In other words, your friend may look like your brother. You may "know" that you're in your house (again, ask yourself, where is this knowledge coming from?) but it doesn't look like your house. If you do notice this incongruity, at first your mind might conjure up a quick explanation. For example, upon noticing a new room in your attic, you might conclude that you just never noticed it, or you forgot it was there. The emotion of excitement might make it more difficult for you to slow down your actions and take time to consider the logical fallacy. Or you might suddenly remember that, oh yeah, I moved last month. These explanations actually overlap with the dreamsign of irregular thoughts. Do not be fooled by these thoughts or swept up by your emotions. Pause and do a reality check.

Context refers to ego role, character role, character place, object place, setting place, setting time, or situation. The same way that forms can blend together in dreams, situations and settings often blend together illogically or impossibly. For example, you may have a dream that you are at work, and your best friend (who does not work there) is there. Perhaps your mother is there too, along with another friend you haven't seen since the seventh grade. You may not notice the incongruity, or again you might come up with some strange explanation for it. For whatever reason, most people's minds are very resistant to the idea that they might be hallucinating.

In these examples, I am attempting to inform you of how your thoughts and emotions react to incongruities in the dream, so that hopefully you do not mistake your dreaming mind's explanations for the truth or become so emotionally invested in the dream plot that you forget to perform a reality check.

An even more effective way of preventing these outcomes is to further prepare yourself to notice your dreamsigns within the dream by doing some analysis while awake. I recommend waiting until you have a month or two of recorded dreams before embarking on this process. Once you have a substantial amount of recorded dreams, read through them and be on the lookout for patterns, to ensure that the dreamsigns you identify are in fact common for you and not an anomaly. There are infinite ways to do this. One way would be to take out four different colored pens, and underline each dreamsign category (inner awareness, action, form, and context) in a different color. Count the instances of dreamsigns in each category to determine which is your most frequent dreamsign.

You can go one layer deeper with this process and identify the most common subcategory of dreamsign to appear in your dreams. For example, perhaps your most frequent dreamsigns are context-based, and specifically you are most likely to dream about a different time or setting in your life. If you often dream that you are back in college even though you graduated many years ago, use autosuggestion and visualization to increase the likelihood that you will become lucid in your next college dream. Think, say aloud, or write down the following autosuggestion phrases: *The next time I see my college campus, I will be dreaming. The next time I see my college roommate, I will recognize the dreamsign and become lucid.* Visualize this happening successfully.

Further, look beyond the confines of these categories to any specific dream occurrence which you know does not happen in your real life. The more specific, the better. For example, the fact that I used to dream about multiplying images of my childhood cat helped me immensely to become lucid. That was a highly specific image, one that certainly would never occur in waking life. If you have any recurring dreams, recurring objects, even recurring ideas, take note of them. Whatever the dreamsign is, make sure to practice autosuggestion (think or say aloud, *when _____ happens/ appears, I will recognize that I'm dreaming*) and visualize a successful lucid dream resulting from this dreamsign.

Beyond the specific purpose of achieving lucidity, taking note of the recurring themes and patterns of your dreams can allow you to become better acquainted with who you are. You may end up finding closure on old wounds, making new psychological connections, and opening up to new ways of looking at your life.

It is possible that analyzing your dreams will cause you to become spontaneously lucid. You will not necessarily have to take note of the dreamsign and perform a reality check exactly as you visualize yourself doing. That said, the next chapter covers reality checks in more depth so that you are prepared to use them if necessary in your dreams as well as in your waking life.

4

Reality Checks

$\mathcal{T}$he term "reality check" refers to the act of checking your reality by performing some kind of mental or physical task in order to determine whether you are awake or dreaming. Reality testing is useful in both the waking and dreaming states. In fact, in the early stages of learning how to lucid dream, performing reality checks in the waking state is of vital importance. The first step in performing reality checks is to ask yourself, right now, whether or not you are dreaming. Your goal should be to perform reality checks as often as possible during your waking life, in order to solidify a habit of questioning reality. Eventually, you will start to perform reality checks in your dreams as well and hopefully become lucid as a result.

Reality checks are especially important at the beginning of your lucid dreaming practice. The more advanced you become at lucid dreaming, the less you will need to perform reality checks in your waking life. Even in your dreaming life, you may eventually forego the need for reality checks. For more advanced and practiced lucid dreamers, your experience of becoming lucid can be nothing more than a feeling. As you have more lucid dreams you will become familiar with all of the myriad differences, big and small, emotional and sensory, between the waking and sleeping states. Eventually, you may get to the point where lucidity emerges suddenly, with 100 percent conviction and without a known cause. This could even happen to you spontaneously without much practice. More often than not though, in the beginning, you will become lucid by noticing some logical incongruity in your environment, which prompts you to perform a reality check.

Sometimes it will occur to you that you *might* be dreaming, but you aren't sure whether or not you are. In that case, you absolutely need to perform a reality check, if not several. Online forums and lucid dreaming books list countless reality-testing techniques, but ultimately it is up to you alone to decide what mental or physical task will most reliably and effectively help you to determine whether or not you are awake.

Some popular reality checks involve attempting a physical feat that is impossible in waking reality, such as flying, floating, pushing your hand through a solid surface, or breathing while pinching your nose. Another category of reality check involves visually surveying the dream environment for inconsistencies or impossibilities. I caution against exclusive use of any particular reality check. Some people claim that in dreams, light switches never work, the numbers on alarm clocks always malfunction, or their hands always look strange. If you find that these reality checks work for you, that is fine. But I caution against using the word "always" to describe the dream state, especially if this information is stemming from your own experience alone. Someone else's experience may differ from yours. For example, I have successfully turned the lights on and off in a dream; therefore it is untrue to say that it's impossible. That is not a reliable reality check for me for that reason. (The light-switch phenomenon was first discussed in a 1981 journal article by Keith Hearne entitled "A 'Light-switch' Phenomenon in Lucid Dreams." The 2001 movie *Waking Life* further spread this rumor.)

My issue with these reality checks is that they could fail. The failure of reality checks to accurately tell you whether or not you're dreaming has to do with expectation. If you think you might be dreaming, but you are on the fence about it and leaning towards thinking you're awake, then you may be unable to push through a solid surface, or fly, or notice anything amiss about your environment. Then you could conclude, falsely, that you are awake, thus losing an opportunity to become lucid. This can and does happen, even to practiced lucid dreamers.

So, then, what do I recommend when it comes to reality checks? First, don't limit yourself to one single type of reality check, and don't ever assume you're awake because you've tested reality in one way and it appears that you are. Try something else.

This is how I recommend you view the process of reality testing: you have begun to suspect you may be dreaming. You are looking for confirmation from the world around you that you are. I recommend in that case simply looking around to see if anything stands out as impossible, illogical, or incorrect. You will probably find something, especially if you are *expecting* to find something.

If you don't see anything amiss, you could try one of the aforementioned tests, such as trying to push through a solid surface, remembering that you should try another test if it fails. You can also perform purely mental reality checks, which I find to be the most reliable option of all. Mental reality checks also serve another purpose besides helping you to become lucid. They help ground you in more logical thinking, something which can help to prolong your lucid dream and help you retain a high level of lucidity, perceptual clarity, and control.

The parts of your brain that handle such logical thinking, conscious awareness, and control generally do not work the same way in a dream that they do in waking life, but you can change that through lucid awareness, by activating regions of the brain which are not typically active during sleep. REM sleep is normally characterized by lowered activity in the prefrontal cortex, and, with that, lowered levels of critical thinking and insight.[1] In lucid dreams, though, there are higher levels of gamma frequency, which is associated with conscious awareness.[2]

One way to mentally determine whether or not you're dreaming is to retrace your steps. Where are you? How did you get here? If you're at work, do you remember driving there? Do you recall waking up this morning? If you cannot account for how you got to where you currently are, you are dreaming.

As a quick aside, I must admit that there are times in a dream when I notice something amiss, and instead of doing a reality check, I conclude that I must be intoxicated. If, in these instances, I take the time to retrace my steps, however, I realize that I'm dreaming. If I fail to do this, it becomes a lost opportunity.

Ultimately, for advanced lucid dreamers especially, lucid dreaming can be achieved through mental analysis alone and without even resorting to retracing your steps. I first had this realization at a pivotal moment in my lucid dreaming practice. The realization occurred during a dream. I was in the kitchen of my childhood home. I had a suspicion that I might be dreaming, but could not decide one way or another. I executed several reality checks, which all failed. I could not fly, or push through solid surfaces. I could not alter the scenery with my mind. Still, I was not convinced that I was awake. For some reason, in this particular dream I was concerned with the possibility that I might in fact be awake, and the potential dangerous or embarrassing consequences which could result from me acting as if I were dreaming. This worry used to plague me when testing reality, but has decreased over the years through practice.

It then occurred to me that I need not commit another physical reality check. I realized that the very fact that I was so unsure whether or not I was dreaming meant I had to be asleep, because I never feel this way while awake. When I practice reality checks in the waking state, they take only a few seconds before I am 100 percent sure of my wakefulness. I do not need to try to fly, or look at my hands, or survey my environment, or retrace my steps because I instantly recognize the waking state. Beginners may not be *quite* as sure and should take the time to genuinely pose this question.

That said, doubting whether or not you are awake seems to be a reliable and defining feature of the dream state. As Stephen LaBerge puts it, in *Exploring the World of Lucid Dreaming*, "You may discover that anytime you feel the genuine need to test reality, *this in itself is proof enough that you're dreaming*, since while awake we almost never seriously wonder if we're really awake."[3] If you are someone who hesitates during reality checks because you are worried about the consequences of thinking you are dreaming when you are not, try to remember that doubt itself is a feature of the dream state. Remember from the section about cautions and caveats that if you can never reliably confirm that you're awake, lucid dreaming may not be the best practice for you to pursue.

To review, reality testing takes many forms. You can test your mind state by performing some action or mental activity. Retracing your steps is a generally reliable option. But most importantly: *when in doubt—you're dreaming.*

In addition to being a means of confirming that you're dreaming while asleep, performing reality checks while awake can increase the odds that you will become lucid at some future time. Every expert you encounter will encourage you, especially in the beginning stages of your practice, to perform as many reality checks per day as you can manage. Working these reality checks into your life can take many forms. You could set an alarm on your phone, or download one of many lucid dreaming apps.

4. Reality Checks

The best reality-check routine should be prompted by something likely to appear in your dreams as well. If you rarely dream about your digital devices, then apps or alarms may not be the best option. You could write a symbol on your hand and do a reality check every time you notice it. You could place post-it notes around your home.

LaBerge writes, "When faced with the challenge of remembering to do something, we can increase the likelihood of success by (1) being strongly motivated to remember and (2) forming mental associations between what we want to remember to do and the future circumstances in which we intend to do it."[4] Identifying what you most hope to gain from lucid dreaming will help you to increase your motivation. Performing reality checks as often as possible during your waking life will increase the number of mental associations you have with the task, increasing the likelihood that one of these associations will emerge while you sleep.

Any reality-checking routine will work so long as it gets you thinking about the concept of lucid dreaming while you're awake, and gets you into the habit of questioning reality. The reason why performing reality checks when you're awake will increase the likelihood of performing one in a dream has to do with the connection between your dreams and your waking habits, thoughts, concerns, setting, and activities.

Dreams can be said to have some overarching qualities to them, across the board for all dreamers. Dreams tend to be emotionally charged, bizarre, and illogical. For many people, dreams have a meaningful and narrative quality, although this feeling can fade upon waking, as your more logical mind tries to put the pieces together. In many cases, the narrative arc appears confusing or disjointed and no longer obviously meaningful after you wake.

There are also archetypal dream topics and symbols such as flying (not just a feature of lucid dreams), nudity in public places, teeth falling out, and the inability to speak or move. All that said, there are individualized aspects to the dream state as well. We often dream of the most important people in our lives, and of the spaces we most frequently inhabit. We dream about our own personal hopes, concerns, and fears, as well as those more overarching fears which humans share as cultural values, such as the fear of being nude in public.

Sigmund Freud coined the term "day residue" to describe his observation that dreams often directly concern events from the previous day. Several teams of researchers have since investigated Freud's theory, and have generally found that research participants do report significant overlap between their dream content and the content of the previous waking day. That is not the only factor at play, however. In 1989, Nielsen and Powell coined the term "dream-lag effect" to refer to the phenomenon of dreaming about waking memories from 5–7 days earlier. What may be occurring, is that, after a week, these dream lag memories are being transferred from the hippocampus to the neocortex for long-term memory storage.[5]

You can take advantage of both day residue and dream-lag effect for lucid dreaming purposes. If your daily life involves several reality checks in various settings, you are more likely to conduct a reality check in a dream. For example, if you often dream of work, and you make it a habit to perform reality checks at work, you may then have a work dream in which the setting reminds you to test your reality. Make a daily habit of checking reality, and both day residue and dream-lag effect will work to your advantage.

It is even possible for an advanced lucid dreamer to reflect on the potential reasoning behind particular dream imagery appearing in her mind, while the dream is still unfolding. I had one such lucid dream recently. Here are some notes I took about it in my dream journal:

> *I dream I have woken up but I notice that my alarm clock looks strange. I test reality by floating into the air, and find that I must be dreaming. My room is underground. I leave it by coming up through a small basement window. I recognize that I am probably dreaming about being underground because of all the subway rides I took the day before. Outside, I'm walking barefoot. I hear music, and think about the fact that my brain is improvising what I'm hearing. I try to concentrate on the melody in the hopes that I will remember it when I wake up. It's springtime outside, with a beautiful blue sky and colorful flowers. I fly for a while, then I stop myself and decide to examine a leaf carefully. I am amazed by the details.*

To sum up, if you have never had a lucid dream before or if you experience them only rarely, it is very important to conduct several reality checks per day. In your waking life, use any technique that allows you to perform reality checks upwards of ten times per day. In the dream state, you will want to experiment with various types of reality checks and find

4. Reality Checks

a method that reliably works. Above all, remember this: If you keep asking yourself whether or not you're dreaming, eventually the answer will be "yes."

	Goal Setting
Week One	Use nightly autosuggestion techniques.
Week Two	Set dream journal goals for next month. These can include how many dreams you hope to remember, or a number of lucid dreams. Start small.
Week Three	Begin to compile a list of dreamsigns from your dream journal.
Week Four	Assess your dream journaling goals and set new ones.

5

Induction Techniques

*A*n "induction technique" is any technique that induces a lucid dream. This chapter discusses the benefits and drawbacks of various induction techniques, ranging from mental visualization practices, to the use of psychoactive substances, to alarm schedules. First, you should know that all lucid dreams fall into one of two categories: wake induced, or dream induced. Stephen LaBerge coined these terms, which are often referred to by their acronyms WILD (wake-induced lucid dream) and DILD (dream-induced lucid dream).

To have a WILD, you must consciously maintain awareness as you fall asleep, such that you enter a lucid dream straight from the waking state. Practicing this technique teaches oneironauts a great deal about how this transition from wake to sleep unfolds. There are countless techniques for achieving a wake-induced lucid dream.

In DILDs, on the other hand, the dreamer becomes lucid from within an already occurring, non-lucid dream. If you have had a lucid dream in the past, without consciously making the effort to enter one from waking as you fell asleep, then you had a DILD. DILDs are much more common than WILDs, since WILDs are only achieved by intentional lucid dreamers, and usually by individuals who have studied this topic in some capacity.

In previous chapters, I introduced you to the simple induction technique of autosuggestion. Saying aloud, writing, or thinking phrases such as *I will have a lucid dream tonight*, *I will recognize that I'm dreaming*, or *The next thing I see will be a dream* are all forms of autosuggestion. This technique can also be paired with any induction method. Autosuggestion will help you increase the likelihood of achieving a DILD. It can also be conducted before attempting to have a WILD.

Knowing that there are two ways to achieve a lucid dream, from within a non-lucid dream or directly from waking, you may wonder if there are advantages to either technique. This is a subjective question and is often debated among avid lucid dreamers. If you are happy with your DILDs, you may opt to continue having lucid dreams that way. Or, you may want to explore WILDs and discover for yourself if these two techniques produce differences in the level of lucidity you are able to achieve.

One advantage to DILDs is that you do not necessarily have to change anything about your sleep schedule or routine in order to have them. By following the advice I have provided so far in this book, you should be able to have a DILD. If you have not been able to achieve a DILD yet, perhaps WILDs will produce better results for you.

How to Achieve a WILD

The goal of a WILD is to transition directly from waking into a lucid dream. For that reason, it is best to attempt a WILD at a time of day or night when you are likely to enter REM sleep. There are a couple of different ways to achieve this. One is to attempt a WILD during an afternoon nap. Another involves setting an alarm for six hours into sleep, at which point you are likely either in or about to transition into a long bout of REM sleep.

Setting an alarm in order to catch a REM cycle is typically known as the "Wake Back to Bed technique," also created by Stephen LaBerge. Six hours is an approximate figure, and if you find that you cannot seem to achieve a WILD using this alarm setting, you may want to experiment with different figures. You can try six and a half or seven hours into sleep. But begin with six hours. See the chart below for reference.

In general, Wake Back to Bed–style WILDs are best suited for individuals who can easily fall back asleep once woken. If that does not describe you, you may need to attempt a WILD during a nap instead.

Once you awake from your alarm, stay awake for about twenty minutes. Write down dreams in your dream journal, if you remember any. Read about lucid dreaming (in this book or elsewhere, but not on a screen, as screens negatively impact your ability to fall asleep). Write or

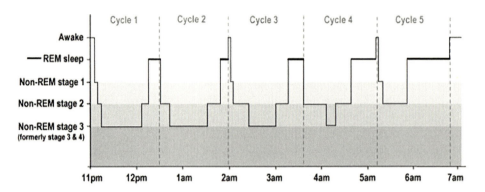

say aloud some autosuggestion phrases. These techniques alone have the potential to lead to a DILD, but there are additional steps to take if you are interested in achieving a WILD.

After twenty minutes, get back into bed. Get into a comfortable, sleep-inducing position. You are attempting the challenging feat of falling asleep while also maintaining awareness as you do so. Meditators will likely have more success than non-meditators, since meditation involves intentionally focusing your awareness. First, you will start to see shifting streams of colored light, or hypnagogic images. "Hypnagogia" is the term used for the transitional state between wakefulness and sleep. Attempting a WILD may be the first time in your life you have ever noticed the features of hypnagogia, though they are always present during this transition.

Eventually, the images you see will become more complete. Instead of streams of light you may see a flash of an image, but it will not last for very long. You will see several of these images appear and disappear before a full dream scene emerges. You may also experience auditory hallucinations, such as voices. Remember that these sounds are the first wisps of dreams. Auditory hallucinations will arise just like the dream images, a sentence or two at a time. Recognize these as hypnagogic hallucinations that will soon morph into a full dream scene.

Personally, I tend to hear dream voices before I see any dream images. It is fascinating to begin to hear the characters of my dreams talking before I even feel myself in a dream! Since I am only half asleep at this point, it is fairly easy for me to rouse myself. On several occasions, I have gotten up only for a moment, to write down an interesting phrase that my mind produced as a hypnagogic hallucination. In fact, I once wrote a series of poems based on these phrases. That is to say, the hypnagogic phase is interesting in its own right and deserves exploration. This is another reason you may want to attempt a WILD—in order to discover what the hypnagogic phase has to offer you if you remain aware throughout it.

What you are trying to do during this hypnagogic state is relax your body and mind enough to fall asleep; at the same time, try to maintain a gentle focus of awareness on the fact that you will soon enter a dream. You want to *notice* the dream as it appears, and recognize it as a dream.

This technique is all about balance, and again, meditators will be familiar with this balancing act. If you try too hard, you will not be able to fall asleep. If you lose your focus, you will fall asleep unconsciously into what is likely to be a non-lucid dream. Be kind to yourself during this process. WILDs are challenging. You will most likely not achieve one on your very first attempt. That is why it's called a lucid dreaming "practice." It takes time.

Remember what you have learned about sleep paralysis. Maintaining awareness as you fall asleep may cause you to fall into sleep paralysis. This is good news, though! If you have managed to reach the stage of sleep paralysis, you are on the edge of a full-fledged dream. Wait until you see a dream scene form around you. You can also speed up this process by focusing your attention on creating dream images. Your brain, in sleep paralysis, is primed for hallucinatory images and sounds. With conscious awareness, you can exert influence over these perceptions and create the kind of dream you wish to have.

Often, from sleep paralysis, the dream scene you experience takes place in your bedroom. This is because you are aware of where your body actually is while you're sleeping and you're likely to create a dream scene based on that initial association. Once the room appears, simply step your dream body out of your dream bed, remembering that you're dreaming, and voilà! You are in a lucid dream.

Drugs

Countless oneironauts have touted their use of certain psychoactive herbs, drugs, and nutritional supplements that enable them to have lucid dreams. I will briefly list some of the most popular choices. This book, however, is chiefly concerned with the natural, mentally focused lucid dreaming practice which need not involve the use of drugs. I do not want to shame or dismiss anyone who finds these substances helpful. Rather, I want to emphasize that they are by no means necessary. You can achieve lucid dreams without the use of drugs, apps, or devices. I reiterate that I am not a medical professional and cannot speak to the long-term health effects of these substances.

Many substances used to "promote lucid dreaming" are utilized because they lengthen REM. Thus, these substances do not specifically induce lucid dreams, but they make lucid dreams slightly more likely due to the fact that you have more dreams after using these substances. I mentioned earlier that readers should avoid cannabis use; however, some people intentionally use cannabis on a nightly basis in order to cause the REM rebound effect when they cease use.

Keep in mind that slightly increasing your chance of lucid dreaming is the most any of these drugs can achieve for you. There is no drug on the planet which can induce lucid dreaming reliably for all users. Individuals vary considerably in how they respond to psychoactive substances. Take a subjective experience like drug use, and combine it with a subjective experience like dreaming, and you're bound to get extremely varied individual responses.

Calea zacatechichi, also known as Mexican dream herb, is so named because it has a historical use among the Chotal of Mexico to enhance dreaming. Like many of the herbs I mention, it can be smoked or ingested as a tea.

Mugwort and melatonin share similar effects, even though one is an herb and one is an over-the-counter drug. Mugwort is the common name for plants in the genus Artemisia. It can be smoked or ingested as a tea. Melatonin, as previously mentioned, is a hormone naturally produced by the brain. It helps regulate the sleep-wake cycle. In recent years, melatonin has grown in popularity as an over-the-counter medicine. People typically take it to curb insomnia. Melatonin increases the amount of time individuals spend in REM, thus causing them to have more dreams and possibly increasing dream recall.

Artemisia vulgaris, also known as wormwood, has a long history of use as a dream enhancer. People ingest it as a tea, smoke it, or even just keep some of the dried plant near them while they sleep.

Overall, the most common effects of any dream herb or drug are increased REM periods and increased dream recall. Individuals using such substances often report increases in dream vividness or dream bizarreness, but I am wary of these conclusions. After all, how do we know that these individuals are not just remembering more of their dreams than they normally do? It seems hard to separate increased vividness from increased recall. Reporting more vivid dreams could just be a matter of remembering more dreams or remembering those dreams in greater detail.

In other words, the drug could be impacting people at the stage of *integrating* dream information rather than at the stage of experiencing the dream. Much more scientific research is needed to say for certain how these substances operate, whether they are worthwhile, and whether they are safe. In any case, no drugs are necessary for a successful lucid dreaming practice. Lucid dreaming is essentially a side effect of these drugs, and by no means the major result of taking them.

The nootropic drug Galantamine is intended as a treatment for Alzheimer's, but individuals have found it to increase the frequency of lucid dreaming. While this early finding proves promising, I reiterate that such drugs are simply not necessary. I do not recommend running such experiments with your own brain until more is known about the long-term impact these drugs have on individuals.

Drugs that produce a calming effect on the user, such as skullcap (scutellaria spp.), valerian root (valeria officinalis) and kava, may help those who struggle with insomnia to get the necessary sleep required for dream exploration.

The subjective connection between well-known historically used dream herbs could be more complex than we currently know. There could be as-yet-undiscovered biological connections specifically to lucid dreaming. What currently proliferates the literature on the topic is accounts of individual experiences. In his book *Dreaming Wide Awake: Lucid Dreaming, Shamanic Healing, and Psychedelics*, author David Jay Brown relayed his experiences with all of the aforementioned substances and several others for lucid dreaming purposes. He reported that mugwort made it hard to fall asleep.[1] If you are interested in experimenting with any of these herbs or supplements, you will want to do additional research beyond this limited information. Even drugs typically used to help individuals fall asleep may end up having an adverse effect on your quality of sleep.

Keep in mind any individual variations, including tolerance to substances. In my view, any one of the aforementioned substances is best utilized as a highly occasional enhancer for a night of dedicated dream practice. As with any dream experiment, if you do choose to utilize any psychoactive substances for your lucid dreaming practice, I recommend taking notes. Include the dosage you took and your method of ingestion, the time you took the substance, the time you went to bed, and of course your dream reports the following morning. That way, you can adjust factors as needed and do not need to run countless trials in order to figure out what works for you. You can determine if the substance led to lucidity, increased vividness, increased bizarreness, increased recall, or all of the above.

Apps

I would like to provide a short, nonexhaustive introduction to the topic of smartphone apps. I will not be reviewing any specific apps, because unlike drugs, which have long-standing histories, any information I provide now is subject to change. Suffice it to say that smartphone users have a myriad of apps to choose from, with various features, including ways to journal on your phone, and randomly timed reality-check prompts. There are also countless sleep-tracker apps, some of which sync data from external devices such as Fitbits, giving users information including when they awoke during the night and how much time they spent in each sleep phase. These devices differ in their accuracy, however. If you need vital information about your sleep for medical purposes, you should seek out a sleep specialist.

Interested readers are welcome to combine the techniques they learn about through this book with the help of a smartphone app. Random reality checks, in particular, are potentially useful. Remember, though, that a fruitful lucid dreaming practice need not be expensive. Always weigh the potential benefit of such apps, drugs, and technology against their cost and compare those benefits with the progress you are able to make on your own. Do not buy into any promise of overnight success. Your lucid dreams come from you—from your psyche, from your mind, and from your effort.

Other Technology

In addition to apps, there is a growing industry of wearable technology designed for the express purpose of increasing lucid dream frequency. As is the case in so many areas of lucid dreaming research, Stephen LaBerge was a pioneer in the field of induction technology with the development of his DreamLight in the mid–1990s. The DreamLight, and nearly all wearable technological devices that followed in its footsteps, relies on the concept of signaling to the dreamer while she is dreaming.

Essentially, inventors in this field are looking for a way to tell the dreamer she is dreaming, while she's dreaming. How do you achieve this without waking the person up? These researchers are tasked with finding an external signal that is strong enough for the dreamer to experience, but not so strong that it wakes her up. Thus far, these signals have mainly been visual or tactile. These methods also require that the lucid dreamer be advanced enough to recognize the signal from within the dream, then use that cue to become lucid.

Keith Hearne experimented with using tactile stimuli to signal to dreamers. In an experiment, he delivered mild electric shocks to sleeping lab subjects' wrists, resulting in half of his twelve subjects achieving lucid dreams.[2]

The DreamLight was the first brand of lucid dream–inducing sleep mask, which, using EEG technology, was able to detect when the wearer entered REM. At that point, the device would flash red lights at the dreamer. This device did not work for all users, as the red light did wake up some individuals. In other cases, the red light might be incorporated into the dream content in such a way that the user did not recognize it as the external signal that it was.

Following the DreamLight, similar electronic devices have emerged in various forms, all drawing on the same principles. At the time of this writing, the NovaDreamer and the REMDreamer are commercially available brands. Advancements have been made since the original Dream-Light, such that dreamers who successfully become lucid are able to turn off the red light by signaling with their eye movements. This is a nice feature, since individuals looking to potentially control certain aspects of their dreams most likely do not want a red light flashing at them periodically, against their will.

The NeuroOn and the Aurora combine features of earlier dream masks with sleep-tracking technology. All these, and undoubtedly others, are available to interested parties. Unfortunately, they can cost hundreds of dollars and may not work on light sleepers who easily awaken from stimuli. Deep sleepers who are also avid, serious lucid dreamers, with some money to spare, are the best candidates for these devices. Luckily, as you have already learned, these technologies are not necessary for you to dream lucidly.

6

Prolonging a Lucid Dream

I am what some dream researchers refer to as a "natural lucid dreamer," because I did not consciously learn how to have lucid dreams. As a young child I held the benefits of a beginner's mind, a child's confidence, and a child's heavy REM periods. Only as a teenager did I begin to consciously try to have lucid dreams more frequently. That said, as a lucid dreaming educator, I am familiar with the common roadblocks for beginners.

You are most likely not a child, and therefore you are not in possession of a child's confidence and long REM phases. The first roadblock you may encounter on this journey is one of dream recall. You can surpass that roadblock by following the advice about increasing dream recall (see chapter 3). Next, you may have trouble keeping a dream journal consistently. This will come with practice. Reading the rest of this book should help you to build your motivation to keep a dream journal, as you read about the benefits of lucid dreaming and all of the activities you can execute once you become lucid.

Some of you may have already overcome these initial roadblocks. You may already be having lucid dreams. The next roadblock, then, and one of the most common and challenging roadblocks to lucid dreaming, is dream duration. In lucid dream classes, discussions, and online forums, I hear this complaint over and over: "As soon as I become lucid, I wake up."

If you have not yet had a lucid dream, don't worry. Do not put too much pressure on yourself. It is possible, as in many skills including meditation, to "try too hard." You need to put effort into this practice, but that effort will be most effective if you are also gentle and forgiving with yourself. Any practice which asks you to form new habits and to look at your world differently is a challenge. This particular challenge, if you stick with it, will have a significant positive impact on your life by expanding your consciousness in new directions.

Those of you who have not yet had a lucid dream will still benefit from reading about ways to lengthen the duration of your lucid dreams. Hopefully, if you have not yet had a lucid dream, you will perhaps be able to avoid the duration roadblock by approaching your first lucid dream with the techniques discussed in this chapter.

For those of you who are currently struggling with the duration of your lucid dreams, first know that you are not alone. Although I personally have not had to overcome the challenge of lucid dreams that end immediately, I have struggled on countless occasions with lucid dreams fading or ending prematurely. I know how frustrating it is to become lucid, and think of all the fun activities you want to attempt or places you want to explore, only for the perceptual elements of the dream to fade.

I recommend here several techniques that you can practice at different stages of the dream and wake states in order to lengthen your lucid dreams. The first technique, positive expectations, you can practice right now. You do not even need to wait until your next lucid dream.

Expectations have important effects on your dreams. You can harness the power of expectation in your lucid dreams by expecting and believing that you can do anything you set your mind to. If doubt, however, creeps in, even subtly, you may prevent yourself from being able to do whatever you set out to do. Understanding how expectations operate can help you to get past the mental blocks set by expectation. Further, this mindset of wholeheartedly believing you can do something before you even attempt to do it will certainly benefit you in your waking life as well.

In the context of dream duration, expectations can serve to lengthen or shorten the lucid dream. Particularly if the very first lucid dream you had was only a few seconds long, you may start to believe that all future lucid dreams will unfold in the same way.

In general, avoid creating negative expectations and mental blocks. Do not say any of the following statements aloud, lest you start to believe them: *I never remember my dreams. I can't remember my dreams. I can't lucid dream. I will never have a lucid dream. My lucid dreams only last a few seconds. I always wake up from lucid dreams. I can't control my lucid dreams. My lucid dreams always become nightmares.*

6. *Prolonging a Lucid Dream*

If you use the word "always," as in *I always wake up from lucid dreams*, you may convince yourself that this statement is true and be unable to move past this mental block. While the statement may have been true so far in your lucid dreaming journey, it will not *always* be true. The same rule applies to any of the above statements. Avoid saying them out loud and thus strengthening their power in your mind. If these statements emerge as thoughts, you can practice positive autosuggestion.

Transform these mental blocks into positive expectations. Think or say aloud one of the following phrases instead: *My next lucid dream will last a long time. Next time I become lucid, I will stay calm.* Try visualizing this. Imagine becoming lucid, perhaps as a result of noticing one of your common dreamsigns. Imagine the lucid dream unfolding precisely how you would like it to. Try to stay positive and fully believe that this is how your next lucid dream will unfold. In particular, try these autosuggestion and visualization techniques immediately before going to bed.

A second technique to increase duration is to remain calm. While strong emotions are commonplace in dreams, a highly intense emotion can be enough to wake you. For example, you may have experienced a prolonged nightmare in which you felt scared the entire time, but you woke up at the height of emotional intensity. It does not matter whether the emotion is positive or negative. Extreme joy, elation, and particularly excitement can wake you from a pleasant lucid dream just as fear can wake you from a nightmare.

Becoming lucid for the first time may be among the most exciting experiences in your life, especially if you have worked toward this goal for a considerable amount of time. It is understandable that you should feel excited. Try, though, to follow the realization that you're dreaming with some deep breaths.

Do not do anything right away. Take a few minutes at the start of your lucid dream to remain calm, collected, and logical. This practice has the added benefit not only of prolonging your dreams, but also of leading to a higher level of clarity and logical thinking.

Dreams fall into one of two clear-cut categories: lucid or non-lucid. You either know you are dreaming, or you don't know. As I have previously argued, this simple definition does need not be muddied through issues of vividness or control of the environment. However, lucidity does exist on a spectrum.

Not all lucid dreams are the same. In one lucid dream, you may realize you are dreaming but still hold illogical and false beliefs. For example, you may know that you are dreaming but believe that some event in the dream is "real," in the sense that it will have consequences for you upon waking. You may have a dream in which you want to have sex, but get hung up on the need for privacy, even though no one can actually see you because dream characters are a figment of your imagination. You may understand that you're dreaming, but fully expect that you will be able to take objects with you to your waking life. All of these would constitute dreams which are on the low level of the lucidity spectrum.

At the high level of this spectrum, you will fully understand not only that you're dreaming, but that your actions will not have consequences for your real life or real body; you will understand that no one can "see" you; you will understand that you are in a hallucinatory realm and that nothing can come back with you to the waking world. At the highest level of lucidity, you will also be able to access considerable information about your waking reality.

For example, in a particularly high-level lucid dream, I knew what day and approximately what time it was (because I had woken up in between alarms and taken note of the time). I knew how old I was and where I lived and worked. This may not sound remarkable, but recall the "context" dreamsigns from the section on keeping a dream journal. Time and setting can easily become fuzzy and hard to recall in a dream, even a lucid one.

Thus, taking the time to ground yourself at the beginning of the dream will help you to remain calm, prevent premature awakening, and also help you to move your lucid dream into the high end of the lucidity spectrum. You will make the most of your lucid dream if you do this at the beginning of it. There is no need to hurry. Take a few deep breaths. Ask yourself some basic questions to help you activate the logical parts of your brain as well as your memories about waking reality. Some options for this include asking yourself what day it is, how old you are, and where you work. You could ask yourself a basic mathematical question, such as what is twelve times seven?

Remind yourself that you are dreaming and all that this implies:

nothing you can see is real in the same sense that your waking life is real; there will be no direct, waking consequences for your actions; you cannot take anything back with you. Remember that your expectations and imagination have a noticeable impact on the dream environment. Remind yourself that you need not become concerned with the plot of the dream, as this is one way you can lose lucidity and thus shorten the duration of your lucid dream.

The practice of retaining lucidity has much in common with the practice of meditation. For that reason, perhaps it should not be surprising that frequent meditators have more lucid dreams than non-meditators do.[1] In meditation, you attempt to focus your attention on something specific such as your breath, and return your attention to your breath whenever you notice that your attention has wandered elsewhere. Your ego will try to suck you back into the plot of your life, in the form of thoughts: ruminating, complaining, planning, fantasizing, etc. Once you notice that this has happened, simply return your attention back to your breath. Try not to beat yourself up for having a wandering mind. In fact, do the opposite. Congratulate yourself for the hard work of noticing and redirecting your wandering mind. This is no easy task.

In a lucid dream, you realize you are dreaming, but dream drama may lead you to lose this understanding. For example, say you become lucid and you immediately decide, without doing grounding exercises, to go find someone with whom to have sex. Perhaps you start a conversation with a dream character, and become emotionally invested in the conversation. This dream character alerts you to some important information: you have to get back to your workplace, your girlfriend is looking for you, you've lost your car. Your concern over this new development may hold so much emotional charge that it distracts you from the fact that you are dreaming, and you reenter a non-lucid dream instead of carrying out any of your plans for your lucid dream.

This act of forgetting looms as a constant possibility in lucid dreams, especially for beginners. For that reason, treat lucid dreaming like meditation. In this analogy, your lucidity, your awareness that you are dreaming, should be like your breath. It is not enough to become lucid once. You will want to return your attention to the fact that you are dreaming whenever you feel your mind drifting too far from this point of focus.

One way to do this is to enlist a dream character to help you. If you are having a lucid dream and someone happens to be near you, you can say, *Remind me that I'm dreaming if I forget.* Saying this aloud may be enough for you to remember. Of course, the other person is not external to you and will not remind you that you're dreaming out of their own volition. You are creating a visual cue for retaining lucidity throughout the dream. Even if you do not feel you are at risk for forgetting that you're dreaming, if you periodically say aloud, *This is a dream*, the act of doing so will help prevent you from forgetting. In any dream, lucid or not, the setting may suddenly change. These changes pose a challenge for retaining lucidity. With new scenery often comes a new dream plot, which may entangle you with unreal, yet emotionally charged problems to solve.

Beyond these largely psychological techniques for lengthening lucid dreams, there are physiologically based techniques. REM sleep, as you've already learned, is named for the characteristic rapid eye movements that accompany dreaming. If you cease moving your eyes in a dream, this can cause the dream to end. Be sure not to stare at a fixed point for too long in a dream, or to close your dream eyes. Either of these actions can cause you to wake up, or to enter a new dream. If your dream environment suddenly changes and you enter a new dream, you will not necessarily carry your lucidity with you, so it is best to avoid this occurrence if you want to prolong a lucid dream.

In contrast, certain actions executed by the dream body can help you to remain in the dream. If you have used all of the above techniques and yet the dream starts to fade, try spinning your dream body. This can help you stay in a dream, but be warned that the environment may change, so be sure to focus on retaining lucidity at the same time as you spin your dream body.

To sum up, the following are ways to prolong and strengthen your lucid dream:

PROLONGING YOUR LUCID DREAMS

1. Ground yourself through breathing, stating your intentions, and asking yourself some logic-based questions such as math problems.
2. Take it slow. Do not do too much too soon. Reserve activities such as flying, sex, or significantly changing anything around you

for when you have sufficiently grounded yourself in a high level of lucidity.

3. Maintain calm emotions throughout. Do not get too excited.

4. Remind yourself throughout the dream that you are dreaming, and consider the implications of this. You may want to enlist a dream character to remind you that you are dreaming.

5. Whenever you remember to do so, say aloud, *This is a dream.*

6. Do not stare at a fixed point for too long, stay too still, or close your dream eyes.

7. If visual elements of the dream begin to fade, try spinning your dream body. Keep yourself in the dream by engaging with it visually, auditorily, or through touch.

Ultimate Freedom

Grounding yourself in a high level of lucidity involves building your understanding of how the dream world operates. Greater and greater knowledge of how your dream world operates will come naturally with time, as you experience more and more lucid dreams and pay more attention to your dreams in general. That said, you will come to this understanding quicker if you recognize it as part of the process of becoming an advanced lucid dreamer.

We all spend far less time dreaming than we do awake. Usually, when we dream, we don't realize that we're dreaming. Therefore, you are likely not very familiar with the dream realm and its infinite possibilities. Reading this book and learning to lucid dream will open up that world to you, but you must be receptive to it. While dreams are extremely strange, while they break from waking reality in countless ways, in some ways they adhere to their own consistent sort of logic. It behooves you to use lucid dreaming to become as familiar as possible with the way your dreams work. This will be a twofold process, wherein the leaps you make forward in understanding the dream world will make it easier for you to become lucid, and your lucidity will inform your understanding of dreams.

To begin with, remember that in dreams, you are alone. You may be surrounded by dream characters or you may be surrounded by friends from your real life, but your friends will not remember the events of your dream. To put it a different way—there are no witnesses to your dream other than you. (Some readers, those who believe that dream characters are real living entities with their own lives and memories, will disagree with me. This is ultimately a matter of opinion as it cannot be scientifically proven one way or another.)

Further, there are no political laws and no social norms in the dream world. We usually are not aware of this, and even in a lucid dream we may forget it, but it's true. Your dreams will still be subject to some types of scientific laws. You will not be able to experience anything that is beyond the realm of human perception. Even in a dream, you will not hear pitches only dogs can hear or see colors undetectable by the human eye. If you have always been blind, you will not see in your dreams, lucid or not. But you can have profoundly novel experiences in lucid dreams that scramble up all perceptual possibilities in strange, new combinations for you. By honing your own conscious awareness and lucid insight, you can take full advantage of the lack of most physical laws, in a seemingly infinite number of ways.

As I said, though, this takes conscious awareness. Even though many dreams involve strange impossibilities, just as often they adhere to our expectations, and those expectations include ideas about the laws of physics. Simple concepts such as cause and effect often function in the expected way in our dreams, based on memories formed in our waking lives. This unnecessary adherence to waking life's scientific laws (such as gravity) robs you of the infinite possibilities available to you in the dream. It takes work to disentangle these unconscious tendencies and open up to other ways of thinking and experiencing in the dream world.

A decade ago, as a teenager, I had a lucid dream wherein I found myself in my parents' backyard. For no particular reason, I decided to pick up a rock and throw it at a tree. It bounced off precisely how one would expect a rock to bounce off a tree, making the expected noise it would make in waking reality. It occurred to me that the rock need not sound like a rock, and that it only did so because I expected it to. Again, I picked up a rock and threw it, but this time I altered my expectations with a more curious attitude. When the rock hit the tree, it made the sound of a dog barking. This may seem like a small difference, but the experience opened me up to a fuller range of possibilities, as well as to a fuller understanding of the role my mind plays in creating the world around me.

This dream reminds me, as so many dreams do, of something I often hear meditation teachers say. In sound-based meditation practices, teachers sometimes ask participants to experience sound without attaching a meaning to it. This is no easy task. The directive essentially asks you to view the world as an infant would view it and as you viewed it before you learned language. Language categorizes sounds, and all perceptions, based on previous experience. Similarly, in the dream world, what we have learned about the world and how it works narrows possibilities, creating boundaries where they need not exist. Lucidity can serve to dissolve those boundaries, and open up possibilities, in much the same way that meditation practice does. The result is a renewed sense of novelty and interest in the place of routine and disinterest.

There are no political or cultural laws, and few scientific ones, in the dream realm. Most of the limitations in your dreams are put there by you. With lucidity, we can gain awareness of the truly infinite freedom and possibility of dreams. They are virtually free of consequences, except for psychic ones. And as long as we behave in accordance with our own personal values, it is likely that those psychic consequences will be positive.

If you've never had a lucid dream, then it's possible you have never in your life experienced freedom of this degree. When you become lucid, take full advantage of that freedom by taking the time to examine and understand it at the onset of lucidity. Just because you understand this now, in your waking mind, does not mean that you will understand it when you are asleep. Therefore, set an intention for a high level of understanding alongside your more general intention to become lucid.

7

Common Mistakes

You are most likely familiar with the following scenario: You wake up. You start to do whatever you typically do first thing in the morning, perhaps picking out an outfit or brushing your teeth. You go out to your car and start to drive to work, but suddenly, you wake up a second time. You realize that what came before must have been a dream, but now you think you must really be awake. You start to get ready and boom! You wake up a third time.

This is known as a false awakening, and it can occur a seemingly infinite number of times in a row. You may, in one of your false awakenings, become lucid by realizing that you are still not awake. Often, the emotion in these dreams is distressing. False awakenings tend to occur late in the morning, approaching the time you have to wake up. You may start to worry about the fact that you have to eventually wake up for real and begin getting ready for work.

As you continue to practice lucid dreaming and increase your awareness of the dream state, you will be more likely to recognize a false awakening as such. At this point in my practice, I tend to instantly doubt that I'm really awake in a false awakening. It may take some time for you to train your mind to do the same.

You may not be able to recognize your first false awakening, but if you have a series of them, you should be able to remember to perform a reality check during the second false awakening in a row. Do not fool yourself into thinking *that was a false awakening, but now I'm really awake.* Perform a reality check.

Be careful not to get swept up in anxiety in these dreams. I tend to have false awakenings in between alarms in the morning. I have three or four alarms to wake me up on work days, and they are spaced ten minutes apart. Sometimes, in a false awakening that turns into a lucid dream, I feel worried that I need to awaken and get ready for work. In these instances I remind myself to pause and consider. I remember that my final alarm has not yet gone off and that I do not need to worry about waking up on time because it is not yet time to wake up. Therefore, I can enjoy the lucid dream and take advantage of it while it lasts.

If you tend to have frequent false awakenings, this is actually great news for your lucid dreaming practice. If you perform a reality check and remind yourself that it's okay for you to remain asleep, then you can use your false awakenings to have lucid dreams. You may also want to consider performing a reality check every single time you wake up in the morning, immediately after you take the time to remember and record elements of your dreams. That way, you will never be fooled by a false awakening.

A false awakening in which the dreamer comes near to the idea that she is dreaming, but does not become fully lucid, is a missed opportunity. Non-lucid false awakenings are by no means the only common lucid dreaming mistakes. The following list of common mistakes is in no particular order.

Dreaming About Lucid Dreaming

At any stage of your lucid dreaming practice, you might find yourself having dreams in which you discuss or think about the concept of lucid dreaming, without actually becoming lucid in the dream. Just last week, I had one of these dreams. In it, I was on a road trip with my parents and my uncle. This dream provided several clues that could have alerted me to my true mental state, had I paused to notice them. First, it is unusual for me to spend time with the uncle who appeared in this dream. This constitutes a context dreamsign, one I missed. Second, we were on a road trip that would last hours, but our final destination was a movie theater. One does not typically drive for several hours just to go to the movies. Lastly, we had not even decided on what movie to see. Eventually, I found myself looking up show times on my phone, and saw that there was a movie about lucid dreaming! Did I perform a reality check, now that the concept of lucid dreaming was front and center in my mind? Sadly, no. I decided I would like to see that particular movie, and continued to engage in the dream plot.

Dreams about lucid dreaming are my most common mistake. I often find myself talking about lucid dreaming in a dream, or I will notice the words "lucid dreaming" written somewhere such as in a book or on a billboard. These are particularly frustrating dreams for me to recall and record in my dream journal the following day.

This phenomenon points to a particular kind of incomplete lucid dreaming practice, one that is more concerned with thinking about lucid dreaming rather than with looking for dreamsigns. Contemplating this particular roadblock reminds me of an underlying argument made by many texts about meditation, dream yoga, and mindfulness. Spiritual gurus of the Buddhist variety tend to state that enlightenment is not something you can come around to through the intellectual, thinking mind. It is an experience. The ultimate goal of dream yoga, for example, is not to have lucid dreams. That is merely a step along the way. The ultimate goal, and the primary practice, is to see and experience the dreamlike nature of existence itself.

Similarly, if one engages in a heavily intellectual lucid dreaming practice, reading and discussing the concept more than actually practicing the techniques, that person will likely experience missed opportunities for lucid dreams because she is too busy contemplating the concept rather than experiencing it. Merely contemplating lucid dreaming with the intellectual mind, without performing daily reality checks, without being on the lookout for dreamsigns, and without engaging in visualization techniques, can lead to this particular pitfall. It is a lot like talking and reading about meditating, but never actually meditating.

Having dreams in which you are discussing, thinking about, hearing about, or reading about lucid dreaming points to the fact that you have successfully moved lucid dreaming to the forefront of your intellectual mind. This shows that you have put in one kind of effort, perhaps in the form of reading this book and thinking about it, but you may need to put in a different kind of effort to actually achieve lucidity.

If you find yourself running into this roadblock, I recommend that you focus your practice on performing reality checks. Try to notice and look for dreamlike elements in your waking life. Visualize yourself noticing a dreamsign and becoming lucid.

You may want to tweak your autosuggestion phrases. In general, it is a good idea to periodically change the wording of the autosuggestion you use. I often tell myself, *I will become lucid in a dream tonight*, but if I use this one phrase for too long it can lead to non-lucid dreams *about* lucid dreaming. When this occurs, I change the wording to something else, such as *I will realize I am dreaming*. I take the emphasis off of the concept of lucid dreaming and instead turn my focus to the act of realization, which is what I'm ultimately trying to achieve.

I Was Dreaming a Minute Ago, but Not Now...

This next roadblock or mistake has much in common with false awakenings but is not exactly the same as a false awakening. If you sleep for eight or more hours, you are having countless dreams. You might remember just one or two, and you may be unsure of the order of these dreams. You probably cannot recall how one dream faded or morphed into another and yet another after that. You may in fact be recalling dreams from different REM phases, such that after one dream ended, you experienced a period of non–REM before your next dream. It is understandably difficult, then, to try to put these memories in any kind of linear order.

You may find yourself in this circumstance: You are in a dream, but you don't know it. You are remembering events from your previous dream, or even two dreams ago. Those events now strike you as illogical. You realize that didn't really happen, that was a dream! You may even tell someone near you about the crazy dream you just had, without ever stopping to think that you might *still* be dreaming.

As you continue to form the habit of dream journaling, you might find yourself having dreams in which you are writing in your dream journal. One way to avoid this roadblock is to do a reality check whenever you record your dreams. It might seem paradoxical or unnecessary to perform a reality check immediately upon waking, but given the prevalence of both false awakenings and dreams about dream journaling—it is a good idea to perform a reality check whenever you find yourself thinking, writing, or talking about dreams. Your mind is providing you with little clues to lucidity, but you need to notice them in order for them to work.

This Almost Feels Like a Dream...

Perhaps most frustratingly, you may even find yourself talking about how dreamlike everything seems, still without remembering to perform a reality check or becoming lucid. This too can be avoided by performing a reality check whenever you find yourself thinking about dreams in any context. It can be hard to believe if you have never experienced this, but it can and does happen.

Here is a personal example. In my dream, I was at work, but rather than the preschool classroom in which I actually work, I found myself in a large conference hall, the kind you might find in a hotel, with long tables and folding chairs. Somehow, at the same time, this conference hall had shelves of records and I soon found myself assisting a gentleman in finding albums by The Clash. I have worked in retail stores before, and my work dreams are often a blend of the various tasks I have done at jobs over the years. Thus, it doesn't surprise me that this dream blended my current job with past jobs, as well as jobs I have never actually had (record-store clerk or hotel employee).

Thus, I appeared to be working in a preschool, a hotel, and a record store, all at the same time. I did not notice this. I was too busy being stressed. I wasn't sure where the kids I work with were, and felt unsure about what I ought to be doing. The fear of being reprimanded, fired, or experiencing some other negative consequence in the work environment is likely what prevented me from becoming lucid. I was simply *too busy* to stop and think about what was going on.

If you learn nothing else from this book, please remember this: *You are never too busy to stop and think about what is going on.* No matter how urgent and emotion-inducing your external experiences are, you can always take the time of a single breath, in and out, to pause and reflect. At the very least, make sure that the stress you are experiencing is *real.* The source of that stress could be literally and completely in your own mind. In fact, most of the time, it is. The solution to a problem created by your mind lies in disengaging with the problem itself.

Again, this is sadly not what I did. I continued running around, stressed and confused. Eventually, I found my students, in a small conference room, seated in rows of folding chairs. Shortly thereafter, I told one of my coworkers about how dreamlike the events of the day felt to me. She conferred that, yes, it did sound a lot like a dream! Still, even then, I did not become lucid. Hence, it is not enough to simply notice the dreamlike nature of events. Doing so must serve as a reminder to perform a reality check.

In conclusion, you can avoid all these roadblocks if you instill the habit of performing a reality check whenever the concept of dreaming arises in your mind. Even if you know you are awake, like when you discuss your dreams or the concept of lucid dreaming with a friend, still perform a reality check. Never skip it. You'll regret it if you do. This is more than a matter of remembering, however. It is a matter both of remembering to perform a reality check, and creating a willingness to stop yourself in the midst of the drama of your daily life.

This is likely a challenge that you will return to again and again throughout your lucid dreaming practice and, in fact, throughout your life. Remember that in spite of the difficulty, this skill is perhaps the most important one for you to cultivate in your lucid dreaming practice, as it will benefit countless areas of your waking life. Being able to stop, take a deep breath, and question your reality in the midst of stress can considerably help to quell the stress, even if the circumstances *are* real.

Take time to ground yourself in reality before you proceed with any action. Remember, too, that even in the waking world, sometimes our most intense stresses, such as fears about the future, are in fact imagined and never come to be. The heightened emotions you experience in difficult circumstances, whether those circumstances occur in waking or dreaming life, do not tend to help you to make a logical choice about how to proceed. Emotions are healthy, natural, important, and vital to our existence—but do ensure that your emotions are not keeping you unconscious.

Losing Lucidity

I already discussed this roadblock at length in the last chapter, but it bears repeating. Remember that just because you have become lucid, that does not mean you will remain lucid. Return your attention to lucidity, just as a meditator would return her attention to the present moment.

Logical Errors

You can know you are dreaming but still believe illogical things. This is not as much a threat to your lucidity as it is a threat to how you are going to spend your time. If you are still in the beginning stages of your lucid dreaming practice, every lucid dream can feel precious (though this is not entirely true, and you should not sweat the small missteps which you are bound to take). It can be frustrating to wake from a lucid dream that was spent in a low level of lucidity full of logical errors. Always take the time to ground yourself logically, in order to prevent the following mistakes.

Here is an example from my dream journal. In this dream, I managed to become lucid, but my thoughts were still highly illogical.

My brother is graduating from school and I've missed part of the ceremony. When I get to the ceremony, my grandmother, who is no longer alive, is there. I do not realize I'm dreaming. Instead, I think that she must be a ghost or that I must be hallucinating. At the end of the dream I do realize I'm dreaming, but only briefly. I think that my parents should be understanding that I've missed the beginning of the ceremony because this is a dream, and it takes a long time to get places in dreams.

As you can see, rather than realizing that I do not need to worry about missing my brother's graduation because the graduation didn't actually take place, I come to the bizarre conclusion that others should understand my actions, given that I'm in a dream. If you have never experienced this kind of illogical lucid dream, it may seem particularly absurd to read about while you are awake and thinking clearly. Do not underestimate how difficult it is to not only become lucid in the first place, but to think clearly and logically in this state.

My perspective on dreaming echoes Allan Hobson's model of the wake-sleep cycle. He differentiates REM sleep, non–REM sleep, and waking, in terms of three variables: Activation, Information Source, and Mode. *Activation* refers to the electrical activity in the brain. *Information Source* refers to where information comes from. In dreaming, the information source is internal; in waking, external. Finally, *Mode* describes the neurotransmitter activity in either state. As explained above, waking life is dominated by aminergic neurons. Sleep is dominated by cholinergic neurons, resulting in very different thought processes.[1]

We are essentially fighting our own physiology when we attempt to think logically in dreams. Much of what scientists have discovered about the neurological activity of the brain during REM sleep confers with our lived experience of that state. For example, aminergic neurons, which are partly responsible for critical thinking, attention, and learning, significantly decrease their activity while we sleep. Aminergic neurons are particularly underactive during REM sleep, while we are dreaming. It's almost as if these neurons are also asleep, and we are trying to wake them up as we awaken to the reality of the situation. Realizing you're dreaming is one step towards thinking critically within the dream, but it is only the first step of many steps you have to take in order to fully harness the potential of the dream state.

Reading about the common logical errors that lucid dreamers make in their dreams should help prepare you to avoid the same pitfalls. One such logical error occurs when dreamers believe that one or more objects in the dream are "real" and can be taken back to the waking realm. These dreams always remind me of a scene in the surrealist novel *The Third Policeman* by Flann O'Brien. In the scene, the main character (who is unnamed) follows two policemen into "eternity," by venturing underground in an elevator. In eternity, time never seems to pass, and any object can be conjured in an instant. The main character spends the entire experience conjuring objects he desires, only to find that the elevator will not allow him back in if he weighs any more than he did when he entered.

Dreams are exactly like O'Brien's eternity: you can have anything you want, right now, but you can't take it with you. In waking, as in death, possessions from the previous world vanish. The saying "you can't take it with you" is as true in the dream world as it is in the waking world. Both worlds are temporary.

Another logical error involves essentially the same premise of taking objects back with you to the waking world, except in this case instead of objects, you try to take back an event. For example, you may have a nightmare in which a close friend dies. Then you may suddenly become lucid, but still decide that your friend *really did die* even though you are in a dream. You may spend the rest of the dream devastated and even planning about how you are going to handle this when you wake up. Lucidity, in this case, is not the savior that it can potentially be in such dreams.

Overall, lucidity will do little to assuage the negative feelings you experience in dreams if you don't fully understand the implications of your own lucidity. There are no consequences in the dream realm. Ultimate freedom exists there. You can have anything you want, but it will be temporary. Events in the dream realm may impact your waking life in the sense that you will have conscious memories and unconscious traces of them, but the dream events cannot touch your waking life in the same way that waking events do.

These points seem obvious now, when you are reading, clear and wakeful. In the dream realm, do not be overconfident in your own beliefs. Remember that it is common to be unsure whether you are awake or not in a dream, and that such doubt does not tend to pervade waking experience. You can be all too easily fooled in the dream realm. Dreaming and waking minds do not function the same; they have different ideas and perspectives. Question everything, up to the point of achieving lucidity, but don't stop there! Keep asking questions. Continue learning as much as you can about the differences between these two equally beautiful but very different worlds.

SECTION TWO

Why Learn to Lucid Dream?

If you have read this far into a book about lucid dreaming, you are likely already convinced of the benefits of learning this skill. The purpose of this section, then, is to connect you with the full range of possibilities for how to utilize your newfound ability. Beyond the myriad of magical activities you can try for pure enjoyment of the dream realm, lucidly guiding your dreaming mind has vast potential for learning about your own psyche, healing old wounds, increasing creativity, and gaining a new perspective on your waking life. Let your personal interests guide your uses for lucidity.

8

Dealing with Nightmares and Anxiety

*N*ightmares are a fact of life, not just for children but for adults as well. With our amygdala in overdrive, unreal events can be among the most frightening events of our entire lives. As I have stated in the earlier section on cautions and caveats, lucid dreams can also be nightmares. Whether lucid or non-lucid, nightmares teach us a great deal about ourselves, including our greatest fears, as well as how best to overcome those fears. These lessons certainly carry over into the waking realm. Dreams provide a virtual landscape for confronting our greatest fears head-on.

Think for a moment about the emotional content of your dreams. How often do you have a dream that is calm or peaceful? How often do you have a dream plagued with apprehension? In my experience, stress is a common dream emotion. In dreams, we are often trying to get somewhere or do something that feels impossible. How often, in a dream, do you actually arrive, safe and sound, at your destination? How often do you achieve the task you set out to achieve? In my own personal experience, dreams are like the middle of a story. Things are happening. There is conflict. Rarely do you get to the very end—the resolution. Lucidity, though, can serve as a means of resolving this story and moving on to a calmer and more enjoyable story, a story you get to write.

While I do sometimes experience the positive emotions of happiness or excitement in my dreams, I don't think I have ever had a non-lucid dream that I could accurately describe as calm, relaxed, or peaceful. Sometimes, though not often, I have portions of dreams that I would call "uneventful," but they are still not precisely relaxed. The only relaxed dreams I've ever had have been lucid ones. From what I've heard of other people's dreams, negative emotions are extremely common. Even if you do not experience nightmares per se, you likely experience dream anxiety or mild dream stress, which can be mediated through lucid dreaming.

Perhaps you are a generally calmer and more relaxed person than I am. Perhaps, then, you do not relate to my descriptions of dream anxiety or stress. It is likely, though, that you experience feelings of clinging to positive experiences and avoiding negative experiences, in your dreams as well as your waking life. I am borrowing the terms "clinging" and "avoiding" from meditation texts. In our dreams, just like our waking lives, we are constantly striving. We are clinging and avoiding. Lucidity in dreams can stop this hamster wheel of thought and action in much the same way that turning your attention to the present moment can ease tension in waking life.

This technique is useful in all kinds of dreams but is especially important for dealing with nightmares. The most effective technique I know for using lucidity to deal with a nightmare involves first remembering that running or fighting will not help you. Those actions are merely more of the same, more avoiding, more striving.

Much of what I argue here echoes the advice of Stephen LaBerge. I have added my own perspective and anecdotes of experimenting with his recommendations for dealing with nightmares.

Facing Your Fears

I am a lifelong sufferer of frequent nightmares. I may owe nightmares a debt of gratitude for connecting me to the world of lucid dreaming. As a child, I often had nightmares in which I became lucid, and I attribute this occurrence to my mind offering a way out of the frightening experience. Unfortunately, though, without proper training, lucidity did little to quell my fears as a child. I fully understood that the monsters or frightening people chasing after me were not real, but nonetheless I felt frightened, and lucidity alone did not dissipate that fear.

Lucidity did, however, open up new avenues for attempting to deal with my fear. I tried to fly away, for example, but found myself completely unable to do so. I knew that I could, theoretically, make frightening figures disappear, but doubts about my abilities tended to become entwined with my fear. This does not surprise me, considering that fear of danger and doubt in your own ability to avoid danger can go hand in hand during an anxiety-provoking experience.

I felt smaller and less powerful than these dangerous figures, even though I fully understood them to be figments of my imagination. Understanding may be enough to transform *your* nightmares into pleasant dreams, depending on your personality and whether you are more or less an anxious person. I am happy for anyone who is able to say *This is a dream; therefore I don't have to be frightened!* and fully believe it. If that works for you, then lucidity alone will be enough to avoid nightmares, and you need only practice the techniques outlined earlier in this book for achieving lucidity.

I want other readers to understand that the knowledge that you're dreaming may not be enough to transform your emotions. For years, my lucid nightmares merely involved trying and failing to fight against frightening beings, until my fear reached an apex and I woke up, considerably troubled and perhaps even afraid to go back to sleep and return to the realm of such disturbing images. Not only was I unable to turn my nightmares into pleasant dreams through lucidity, but, as discussed previously, lucidity sometimes turned a pleasant dream into a nightmare.

It was not until I read *Exploring the World of Lucid Dreaming* and other books on this topic that I was able to use lucidity to turn a nightmare into a pleasant dream. The general consensus among dream experts, post–LaBerge, is that fighting against your fears will not work. It is not that I was failing to execute proper flying technique to escape these enemies. In a calm lucid dream, I can execute flying with consistent success, because I am able to overcome my doubts and hone my expectations. In a lucid nightmare, however, the fear response can be too powerful to overcome.

The fact is that escaping was entirely the wrong route for me to take. What does it mean to *escape* a figment of your imagination, when you are the one conjuring up both the fearful emotion as well as its visual manifestation? Let's say you successfully "escape," to another realm of the dream world. You fly away from your house and land at the park across town. What exactly is to stop the enemy from reappearing? In other words, what is to stop your *fear* from returning, and, with it, the visual manifestation of that fear?

Overcoming a nightmare is not about physically escaping or defeating an external enemy. Fear is an emotion. It can travel with you everywhere you go. Overcoming nightmares is about transforming your own attitude from one of fear, to one of some other emotion, such as acceptance or true understanding. This true understanding is not merely the understanding that the fear is not "logical," and the visual manifestation of it "imagined." It is a deeper understanding of the underlying reason for your fear and the reason behind its particular manifestation. It is the understanding that, although you are afraid, you will face your fears. It is further the understanding that perhaps you need not fear what you think you need to fear. In a lucid nightmare, bravery is more important than power. You do not need to be powerful or unstoppable: you just need to be courageous.

Theoretically, you could sit with your fear and try to transform it directly into another emotion. I have attempted this before. In one lucid nightmare, I found myself in a maze of dark, narrow corridors. There was no specific enemy to escape, defeat, or confront, just a pervasive feeling of claustrophobia. I tried to conjure up images of wide open space and to cultivate positive emotions, but I could not overcome my fear in order to do so.

In your waking life, when you ask something like *What am I afraid of?*, you learn a good deal about your underlying motivations and what matters most to you. You become better acquainted with the inner workings of your ego—what it clings to and what it rejects. In the dream world, confronting your fears often causes those fears to dissipate almost immediately.

The best way to deal with your fear in a nightmare is to confront it directly. Gently approach the frightening dream figure or image, remembering that it is only the visual manifestation of an emotion, and ask it some variation on the following questions: *What do you want?* and *Why are you here?*

At first this may seem counterintuitive. It may seem absurd to walk *towards* a murderer, for example, rather than run from him. The efficacy of asking your dream enemies what they want and why they are there is best explained through example. After keeping a dream journal and practicing lucid dreaming for many years, I started to have an increasing number of lucid nightmares when my lucidity itself started to trigger these frightening experiences immediately.

In one particular dream, I became lucid within my childhood home and decided to walk down the street and merely observe. Soon after, I started to feel anxious, sensing a presence behind me. I turned around and saw a horse. (There is a horse barn on this street in real life.) At this time in my life, many of my nightmares involved being chased by wild animals. It is worth noting that I do not have this type of nightmare anymore. It is possible that through confronting this fear head-on I was not only able to transform this specific dream's emotional content—I was able to achieve closure on this imagery and put it aside once and for all.

When I saw the horse, I was extremely frightened, even though I knew I was dreaming and that none of my perceptions were real. Luckily, I remembered the advice which I had read, and I asked the horse what it wanted. The horse didn't answer me in words, but I understood telepathically that it wanted me to ride it. I got on the horse, which no longer scared me, and began to ride. I never would have thought to seek out a horse in a dream. This was not anywhere on my list of planned lucid dream activities. I found riding it to be a thrilling activity, worthy of any lucid dream, and one which I recommend to you to try. Soon after I began to ride it, the horse lifted off the ground, and we both flew into the sky. This was also unplanned, and not my idea. It happened spontaneously.

You may be continually surprised, as you explore the dream world lucidly, by how much you *do not* directly determine about your dreams. While on the one hand, lucidity and dream analysis teaches us the role that our thoughts and expectations play in the unfolding plot of our dreams, careful observation will also teach you that dreams are full of surprises such as these. Not everything that happens in a lucid dream will be your own idea. Whose idea, then, is it? That's a question for neuroscience as well as philosophy.

I am grateful for the spontaneity of this dream, which only arose after I engaged in a dialogue with my fears. The visual manifestation of my fear ended up suggesting dream activities I never would have independently tried. This lucid dream was infinitely more interesting than the majority of my lucid dreams, in part because I relinquished a great deal of the supposedly important "control" that one is able to exert in such dreams.

Instead, I let the dream guide me where it felt it needed me to go. I let fear show me what it wanted to show me, and I was forever changed.

If I had given in to fear, if I had run from the horse, I never would have ridden it into a gorgeous, dream sky. Instead, I would have continued to have dream after dream about being chased by wild animals. I believe this is a scenario comparable to shying away from sleep paralysis rather than letting go of control and seeing sleep paralysis as an opportunity rather than a situation to be avoided.

This experience taught me that I have the ability to turn a dream from frightening to beautiful, all through facing my anxiety. I have every reason to believe that the same logic applies to the waking realm. I am in fact grateful for lucid nightmares because they have taught me a great deal more about my consciousness than my happy lucid dreams have.

Connections to Waking Anxiety and Wakeful Hallucinations

In previous chapters I likened the fear of nightmares and sleep paralysis to the fear experienced in waking anxiety. The knowledge of your own ill logic does not make the emotion disappear. If it did, no one would experience anxiety. Similarly, I would like to further make the comparison between dream experiences and hallucinogenic or psychedelic drug experiences.

Some dream enthusiasts take issue with the use of the word "hallucination" to describe the dream realm. If you subscribe to the belief that dream and waking life experiences are each equally "real," you may disagree with my use of the term "hallucination." I need to explain my perspective on this debate and my reasoning for using this word as a descriptor of the dream state. According to the *Oxford English Dictionary*, a hallucination is "an experience involving the apparent perception of something not present."

This definition leaves a few questions to be answered. One could ask, present *where*? One could also ask, present *for whom*? Ultimately what this means is that the hallucinatory perception is not externally present in a tangible way in the waking, sober realm, such that anyone in proximity to the source of the perception would also perceive it. I am not arguing that hallucinations, whether drug-induced or dream-induced, are not "real," or even that they are not "present." These perceptions are real. They are present within the mind of the hallucinator, which is as significant a place for them to take place as any. All perception ultimately takes place in the mind anyway.

However, the perceptions are not necessarily present for anyone else in proximity to the dreamer or the hallucinating individual. Accounts of shared dreams and shared psychedelic experiences do exist, but they are the exception, not the rule. We are each free to believe or not believe these experiences. In any case, even if shared hallucinations are possible, in the form of either shared dreams or overlapping drug experiences, I would still consider these experiences to be hallucinations based on the dictionary's definition. Based on the definition, I choose to include dreams in the overarching category of "hallucination."

You are free to consider dreams to be hallucinations, or to disagree with that terminology. In any case, I find that there are many connections between hallucinogenic drug experiences and dreams. For one thing, overcoming fear in the dream world has much in common with the challenge of overcoming fear during psychedelic experiences. Readers with a background of psychedelic experimentation will be able to use what they have learned during these experiences. The comparison may also clear up some confusion among readers who are still skeptical that lucid dreams can be unpleasant or nightmarish. In response to the claim that no one should fear the unreal, I would ask you to imagine making that argument to a person in the throes of a hellish hallucinogenic trip.

"Don't worry, it's not real" holds little weight for a person in the midst of this experience, who may be experiencing visceral, physical pain or discomfort as well as troubling visual perceptions and thoughts. I will provide one additional perspective before moving on. Author and lecturer Terence McKenna often said, "Nature loves courage." He typically made this statement in the context of psychedelic drug use, but it applies to the dream world as well. In fact, he alluded to dreams when he said,

> Nature loves courage. You make the commitment and nature will respond to that commitment by removing impossible obstacles. Dream the impossible dream and the world will not grind you under, it will lift you up. This is the

trick. This is what all these teachers and philosophers who really counted, who really touched the alchemical gold, this is what they understood. This is the shamanic dance in the waterfall. This is how magic is done. By hurling yourself into the abyss and discovering it's a feather bed.[1]

You are part of nature. The dream world is a natural one, and it too loves courage. Your psyche loves courage. It is simply not courageous to transform a dragon into a bunny rabbit or to escape it by flying away. In doing so, you are not confronting your fears, you are battling them. You are making your fears into tangible enemies and engaging them in a power struggle. Thus far in this chapter I have argued for you not to do so because you are unlikely to win this battle. Beyond this initial point, it's worth noting that battling your fears is less psychologically lucrative, less courageous, than gaining a greater understanding of your fears through engaging them in a conversation.

If you are able to battle your fears through physical means and win, then you are not truly afraid to begin with. The truly brave thing to do is not to "defeat" your fears but to face them completely, see what they are, ask what they want from you, and listen carefully to what they have to say.

How to Wake Up from a Dream

Given everything I've said so far, you will not be surprised to hear me argue that using lucidity to wake up from a nightmare is a cowardly approach. I understand the temptation to escape to the more comfortable and predictable realm of waking life, but I must caution against it.

Remember that waking life is comfortable not because it is less dangerous. In fact, it is undeniably more dangerous than the sleeping realm. Comfort grows out of familiarity. We spend one third of our lives asleep and dream for a fraction of that time. The majority of our life is spent in the waking realm, making it the more familiar and safe-*feeling* of the two realms. The unbalanced ratio of time spent in either state may also play a role in the fact that most human beings value waking life more and believe their waking experiences to be more important than their dreaming ones.

If you opt to awaken from your lucid dream, likely you will find yourself in your comfortable, warm bed with nothing immediately to fear. You will succeed in escaping the unfamiliar and frightening dream realm. But then what? You may wake up with the emotion of fear still coursing through you, and while waking can provide temporary relief, you will have to face your fear of sleep all over again when faced with the decision of whether or not to go back to sleep. Likely you will have to fall back asleep, perhaps fearfully, and will end up precisely where you started, having gained nothing. You will have wasted the opportunity for a lucid dream.

That said, I might as well tell you some of the techniques that can cause you to awaken from a dream. For one thing, you may want to consciously wake from a lucid dream in order to record an important realization or creative idea you had in the dream. As I stated in the chapter "Prolonging a Lucid Dream," staring at a fixed point for a long time can cause you to awaken. Closing your dream eyes can also cause you to awaken, though it is equally as likely to simply change the dream scenery to that of a new dream. It is important to remember these two facts in the context of the next chapter, since certain activities could cause you to accidentally stare too long at a fixed point or close your eyes and end the dream.

9

Activities to Try
in a Lucid Dream

O nce you achieve lucidity a few times, you may start to wonder how you can best take advantage of your new mind state for spiritual growth, psychological healing, exploration, or simple fun. In this chapter I will provide suggestions and tips for successfully engaging in particular activities. Just as there is a spectrum of lucidity, there is a spectrum of difficulty when it comes to lucid dream activities. You will easily achieve some right away. Some require more practice. Do not feel obligated to try anything on this list. Your dream world is your own personal playground, temple, and library. These are mere suggestions.

Flying

Flying is often where dreamers start. There is a strong cultural and psychological connection between dreams and flying. Even in non-lucid dreams we sometimes find ourselves flying. Perhaps it is completely natural, then, that so many people try flying as their first lucid activity.

I have cautioned in previous chapters against trying to fly right away, especially in your first lucid dream, because if you aren't careful this can lead to too much excitement and cause the dream elements to fade. Remember to take a few moments to ground yourself in the dream world and increase your lucidity before trying any of the activities on this list. The time you take to ground yourself will pay off by lengthening the duration and quality of your lucid dream.

Once you have sufficiently grounded yourself in logic as well as confidence in your abilities, you can try any number of flying techniques.

You can imagine your dream body floating up off the ground. You can put your hands in front of you, Superman-style. The specific "physical" technique does not matter. Remember, this is a mental skill, not a physical one. Personally, when I fly in dreams I simply float up into the sky. While it is up to you, I do not recommend flapping your arms like wings as this will solidify in your mind the erroneous feeling that flying is a matter of physical effort rather than mental imagination.

For many dreamers, starting to fly comes easily, but controlling the speed, duration, and trajectory of your flight can prove difficult. It takes a delicate balance to stay afloat in the sky. First, believe that you can. Remember the importance of expectations. Expect to have great control over the speed and trajectory of your flight. Even the slightest doubt can cause you to fly too fast, too slow, or with little control over your speed and direction. Even a seemingly harmless thought such as *I hope this goes well* can wreak havoc with your success. Nature loves courage. Be courageous.

To give you an example of the power that doubt has to interfere with your success, I have had many lucid dreams in which I was flying along just fine until doubt appeared. I might have a thought such as "*Wow! This is going really well! I hope I don't start to fall....* Then, as quickly as the thought came, I started to fall.

Of course, it's not easy to control our thoughts. It is particularly hard, in fact impossible, to intentionally *avoid* certain thoughts. You will have more success honing your confidence and your expectations. Rather than trying to avoid doubt, try to cultivate confidence. Focus on the positive. One way to do this is through visualization while awake. Identify the dream activity you are most interested in executing, and imagine this activity going exactly as you would like it to go. Focus on your belief that you can do it. Fully expect that you will have success.

In addition to staying positive, keeping an open and curious mind will help you to come up with solutions in the dream realm. Always remember that physical effort makes no difference whatsoever. Your physical body is paralyzed in bed. You may feel your body as realistically as you do when you are awake, but remember that this is an illusion. Think outside the box. Think outside the *body* when trying to come up with solutions to dream challenges.

Dreams in which the dreamer struggles to walk, talk, run, or fly, are incredibly common. Dreamers typically react by doubling their efforts, but it makes no difference! Try a different tactic. In the case of flying, use your imagination. If you are attempting to fly over a mountain range, you can focus your attention on the landscape rather than your body. Focus your imagination on what the landscape will *look* like rolling past you at your preferred pace. Imagine what your body will *feel* like flying with complete control. Attempting to flap your arms harder and harder will likely just cause more difficulty. Imagination, confidence, and mental focus are key to any dream activity.

Similarly, in lucid dreams in which I am having trouble talking, I opt to communicate in some other way. I first realized this as a possibility when I was trying to teach myself American Sign Language. Learning this new language helped me understand that communication need not be oral. This perspective followed me into my lucid dreams, wherein I found myself either signing, or forgoing language altogether and communicating with others telepathically. This creative work-around was much more successful than the frustrating action of trying to speak when my voice simply would not comply with my attempts. Have an open-minded attitude towards problem solving in your lucid dreams, remembering the infinite possibilities of this realm.

With all of the following activities, keep your spirits high. Just as achieving lucidity in the first place took practice, lucid activities take practice. You will develop your own techniques over the years.

Sex

Sex is also high on the list of lucid dream activities for most people. If you are not interested in dream sex or find the topic unsavory, feel free to skip this section.

Increased blood flow to the genitals is a physiological characteristic of REM sleep. For that reason, even if you do not intend to seek out sex in your lucid dreams, you may feel differently when you're asleep.

Sex is among the more difficult dream activities, though it is by no means the most difficult. To successfully have sex in a lucid dream, you may have to execute other, equally difficult dream activities such as making people appear. Let's say you become lucid in a dream but there are no people around, or no people to whom you are attracted. In that case you have to begin with the difficult task of finding an attractive person.

Try to expect to find someone. For example, if you are in a building, expect to find an attractive person around the corner. Slightly changing the dream scenery by walking to a new room with the expectation of finding people there tends to be easier than building the image of someone up from scratch.

Once you have an attractive partner, what comes next is the issue of location. It is common to spend an entire lucid dream wasting time looking for a "private" place to have sex. Just remember, you are in the most private place imaginable: your own mind! No need to get a hotel here. That said, even knowing this, it can be difficult to get past. It sure *feels* like you are having sex in front of other people, even if they are dream characters. You may even begin to doubt your own lucidity, thinking, *but what if I'm awake! I'll get arrested!* If necessary, do another reality check just to put your mind at ease. Do not waste time looking for an ideal place. Once this worry has crept into your mind, it can become a mental block, and you may never find an empty room. You could easily waste an entire lucid dream this way.

It is better to put in the mental effort of getting past your embarrassment. This effort will benefit you in future dreams. Over time, you will likely become more familiar with the dream world and understand that it is a private realm of experience.

As far as the physical act of sex in the dream is concerned, like flying, it is a mental act more so than a physical one. It is possible for the person you're having sex with to suddenly look different or even to disappear. The dream environment is always in flux, which is a factor in all dream activities. During dream sex, you have to be particularly careful not to close your dream eyes or stare too long at your sex partner, since, as you have learned by now, either of these actions can cause the dream elements to fade. Periodically look elsewhere.

Some dreamers have difficulty achieving orgasm in a dream. Others wake up mid-orgasm. If you haven't used a lucid dream to intentionally have dream sex before, try to have an open mind about the outcome, as different people have different experiences.

In *Dreaming Wide Awake*, David Jay Brown notes that "when a man achieves orgasm in a lucid dream his physical penis doesn't actually ejaculate (like in a wet dream), and his heartbeat isn't significantly elevated."[1] You may notice, as I have, that women are conspicuously absent from Brown's statement. Sadly, women are often conspicuously absent in the scientific literature on this topic. While it is more difficult for an individual with a vagina to know for certain whether or not a physical orgasm occurred, scientific exploration of the matter is by no means impossible. Sleep researchers should explore this question.

For now, all I can say is that, no matter your genitalia, you might not technically be having a physical orgasm even if you feel as if you are. That said, this fact is probably of more interest to scientists than it is to lucid dreamers who are just trying to have a good time.

Talking to Dream Characters

Talking to dream characters is one of the easiest lucid dream activities, as long as your dream is not devoid of dream characters. Several philosophical questions arise when we consider the strangers who appear in our dreams. To begin with, are they based off of people we have seen in passing in our waking lives, or do our brains conjure them from scratch? It does not seem to me that there can be any way to answer this question with certainty.

Some argue that dream characters remain in the dream realm independent of us, or believe that they are people in the real world who are also dreaming while we are dreaming. With billions of people on the planet dreaming every night, how could we ever know for certain?

Whatever your opinions and beliefs about dream characters, understand that you can learn a good deal about the dream world by interacting with these characters. You can explore your own philosophical beliefs about dream characters by asking them if they are "real," if they are also dreaming, and so on. You can do this for mere entertainment or as a more serious inquiry.

Practice for Waking Life

Lucid dreams provide you with a virtual reality space in which to practice skills. Researchers have already proven that sleep is essential to memory consolidation as well as emotional regulation and creative problem solving in your waking life. Getting a good night's sleep is an excellent idea before any important performance or activity. If you are able to add lucidity to the mix, you can *intentionally* practice in your sleep. This ability to guide the content of your dreams is almost like being able to add hours to your day!

Researchers Erin J. Wamsley and others conducted a study in 2010 that further clarified the specific role of dreams in memory consolidation. Research participants were tasked with navigating a virtual maze. Half of those participants took a ninety-minute nap, while the other half did not. After either resting or watching a video, all participants completed the maze task a second time. Those who napped performed much better on the second maze attempt than those who did not nap. What's really remarkable, though, is that those who dreamt about elements of the maze performed *ten times better* than their napping counterparts who dreamt about other topics.[2]

This study helps to demonstrate what many advanced lucid dreamers intuitively know to be true. Not only does sleep assist us in consolidating memories; what we dream about also has an impact on which memories become consolidated and to what degree. The implication is that, through awareness of your own dreaming, you have the power to guide the unconscious mind to specifically work through the problems that your conscious mind considers most important. Through lucid dreaming, and especially through planning ahead of time what you want to do in your lucid dreams, you can utilize sleep and dreams more intentionally. In lucid dreams, you can decide to practice specific tasks, and as this maze study demonstrates, dreamed practice can have a real, significant impact on waking performance.

What kinds of activities lend themselves best to dream practice? Anything that can be mentally rehearsed. I used the initial examples of sports and music because I believe these are ideal examples of hobbies that you can practice in a dream. If you have a piece of music memorized, you can sit and visualize yourself playing the piece perfectly, and will likely gain some confidence for having executed this visualization. Taking this visualization to the dream realm will make the experience feel entirely real.

Similarly, if you are an athlete, whether you are a ballet dancer or a soccer player, you can practice the most challenging athletic moves in the dream space. While it isn't "real," and you won't be gaining muscle tone from this practice, you will feel as if you are really executing these feats. You will be signaling to your brain that this activity is what you want to improve upon through dreamed rehearsal.

As always, I recommend taking the time to ground yourself in a highly lucid dream before attempting this. A lucid dream in which you intend to practice for a performance could easily slip into a non-lucid dream if you aren't careful. Additionally, you need to have a great deal of self-confidence for the performance to go well in the dream—just as you do in real life. Don't rush yourself.

You can also utilize the dream to practice for something less physical, such as a speech or a difficult conversation. Let's say you are nervous about broaching some challenging topic with your romantic partner. You can use the dream space to practice what you want to say, and practice responding to your partner's questions and responses. Perhaps new factors will arise in the dream conversation which you were unable to anticipate in your waking rehearsals.

It is worth noting that nearly all of these rehearsal activities involve making objects or people appear. If you want to practice your guitar, or play soccer, or have a conversation with your partner, you will need a guitar, a soccer ball, or your partner to be there in the first place. You might need to conjure up an entire scene, as in the sports example.

Making People or Objects Appear

Whatever your lucid dreaming goals, you may find yourself in a position where you want to make an object or a person appear. Let's say you've decided to indulge in some unhealthy behaviors in the dream realm, because they will not affect your real body. You will have to find a way to make that chocolate cake, or cigarette, materialize.

9. Activities to Try in a Lucid Dream

I probably sound like a broken record for saying that you first need to ground yourself in a highly lucid dream. I am repeating myself because this tip applies to all lucid dreams and lucid dream activities, but for slightly different reasons in each context. In this context, if you were in a lucid dream on the low end of the lucidity spectrum, you might get bogged down looking for a bakery or a convenience store.

Even lucid dreams can follow the typical dream-plot formula, wherein you are constantly chasing after something you can't find. From your life of dreams thus far, you are most likely familiar with this formula. Say you find a bakery, but it's closed, so you go looking for another. The next one is open, but only sells vanilla cake, or the man behind the counter refuses to sell to you, or you've lost your wallet. This is just how dreams tend to go. Lucidity offers us an opportunity to break out of this hamster wheel of effort, but only if we are fully lucid and able to think creatively as well as logically, in this realm where a different kind of effort is needed than in waking life.

First and foremost, remember that you are trying to *expect* and *imagine* these objects and people into existence. Remind yourself of the way that the dream space seems to inherently thwart your intentions, and look for clever ways around this. In the above example, if the bakery is closed, open the door anyway! The door is locked? Walk through it! You lost your wallet? You don't need it. The man won't sell to you? Convince him. You probably do not want to fight this dream character or steal the cake and run away, as you could get swept up in a new, non-lucid dream plot as a result. Just remember at every turn that the bakery, the salesman, and the cake are all figments of your imagination. For that reason, you really don't need to find a bakery. You could find a delicious piece of cake in your pocket, so long as you 100 percent believe and expect it to be there.

The best technique for making objects and people appear most likely depends on your individual mind and your particular abilities. Personally, I have considerable difficulty visually imagining things in my waking life, and while my dreams are extremely vivid, I still have trouble creating objects from scratch. But if you are an artist, or a highly visual person, think about how you can solve this problem visually. You could grab a paintbrush and paint a chocolate cake to eat. You might be able to make someone appear just by imagining what they look like. Just be sure to remember the importance of expectations, confidence, and belief.

Changing the Scenery

Perhaps you don't just want to find a particular person or object, but wish to visit a specific place. Changing the scenery is more challenging than making one specific object appear. While you are the major source and creator of your dream, and it is stemming from your imagination and expectations, it can be difficult to overwrite the existing scenery.

Creating a new scene essentially involves dissolving the current scene in some way, and depending on the technique you use to do so, this can cause instability, which can lead to waking up or to entering a non-lucid dream. You can try to approach changing the scenery in the same manner as making objects appear. In other words, you can walk through a doorway expecting to find a soccer field on the other side. This might be difficult, because it can be hard to fully wrap your mind around the truly endless possibilities of the dream state. It's one thing to expect to find a piece of cake in your pocket. It's another thing to expect to find a soccer field in the next room. Your mind, which spends most of the time awake, may doubt this possibility and cause you trouble. It takes practice to fully understand the ultimate freedom of the dream state and to overwrite your expectations, which are based on the rules of the waking world.

The most popular technique for changing the scenery in a lucid dream (another technique created and popularized by Stephen LaBerge) is through spinning your dream body. By spinning your dream body, the landscape will become blurry in your vision, and when you steady yourself, you can create a new scene. While spinning your dream body, you want to concentrate your attention on imagining the scene you want to create.

Using the soccer field example, think not only about what soccer fields look like—try to imagine the grass smell and the sound of people running. Another advantage to spinning your dream body is that this technique lessens the likelihood of waking up. Changing the scenery creates instability in the dream, but by spinning your dream body, you remain connected to your dream body rather than your waking one. This keeps you grounded in the dream even as you change it.

Meditation

As discussed throughout this book, there is an undeniable connection between the practices of meditation and lucid dreaming. These metacognitive activities connect you with the inner workings of your own mind.

Lucid dreaming allows you to harness the hours of your life you spend asleep. While dreaming has inherent value, regardless of whether or not we are lucid, lucidity allows you to influence how you spend this time. Just as meditators continually redirect their attention to their breath and to the present moment in waking life, you can do this in your dreams as well.

Meditating in your dreams may help to solidify in your unconscious your intention to live a more mindful and present-focused life. If you are struggling to maintain a regular meditation practice in your waking life, lucid meditating provides another realm in which to try. Perhaps you will have wildly different meditative experiences in the dream state than you do in the waking state. Meditating in a lucid dream will certainly teach you a great deal about how your mind works in the dream state.

So, how exactly should you meditate in a lucid dream? You should be able to conduct the same style of meditations in the dream world as you do in your waking life, with a few alterations. If you like to do walking meditation, wherein you focus on your breath and the feeling of your body as you walk, there is no reason you cannot do the exact same practice in a lucid dream. If you like to sit in lotus position on a cushion on the floor and close your eyes, you could try this in a lucid dream, but you might wake up! It is best to keep your eyes open and occasionally moving, but that is the only change you will have to make to your practice.

Here is an example from a lucid dream in which I decided to meditate. This example also serves to demonstrate the ways in which sleep paralysis, false awakenings, and lucid dreams function in tandem. Often sleep paralysis will turn into a lucid dream, as in the following example, but other times, lucid dreams can fade into sleep paralysis.

I have sleep paralysis. I try to relax into a lucid dream but end up having a false awakening. I get up out of my bed and start walking around the house. I'm at my parents' house. Outside, in the driveway, I see a purple minivan. I conclude that I must be dreaming because the minivan should be teal instead of purple. I decide to try a walking meditation. Perception becomes unstable immediately. I say to myself: Breathing in, I know I'm dreaming. Breathing out, I'm stable. I repeat this over and over and am able to restabilize my perception with confidence.

Something funny to me about this particular dream is that I was able to become lucid because my mother's minivan was the wrong color. What I did not notice at the time was that she has not driven a minivan in about twenty years. This is fairly typical of how the brain can think critically enough to become lucid, but will still miss red flags that are humorously obvious to the waking mind.

Meditation teachers often spend a good deal of time coaching meditators on what to do with their bodies while they meditate. Whether the meditator is sitting, walking, or lying down, focusing on the sensations of the body tends to be a central and integral part of meditation practice. In a lucid dream, keep in mind that you do not even need to *have* a body. If you wish to focus on the sensations of your dream body, this could be fruitful and interesting. Or you could instead choose to exist as something else entirely: an animal, or a tree, or a cloud. You could transform your body into a simple point of awareness.

It is hard to say what impact these alterations would have on each individual's meditation practice, but be aware that you have these options at your disposal. Perhaps relinquishing your body altogether will have an interesting effect on your mental awareness.

Exploring and Observing

Exploring and observing the dream state is one of the simplest and easiest lucid activities, and yet it is my personal favorite activity for lucid dreaming. I have intentionally placed it towards the end of this list because I think people roughly proceed in a certain order with dream explorations. Most oneironauts will try something like flying first. Sex also has a strong draw for obvious reasons. Later, dreamers may decide to use flying to explore and see as much of the dream world as possible. Observing the dream as it is without interfering or moving about in the space does not always occur to oneironauts as a possibility. It is often once we have had our fill of dream flying, sex, indulgence in food and sensory pleasures, and scene changing, that we may decide to simply observe things as they are without exerting control over the dream.

I want to alert you to this option, which, at this stage in my lucid dreaming practice, happens to be my preferred activity. This activity somewhat stems out of meditation. Through meditation I have come to value the act of observing my mind in stillness and awareness. As a logical conclusion, I have begun to do the same in the dream state. When I talk about observing the dream state, though, I do not mean exactly the same thing as meditating. There are similarities and differences. Rather than observing your thoughts or centering your awareness around your breath, I am recommending that you try observing your dream *perceptions* without trying to direct them in any particular way. Remember, though, that your dream perceptions are inherently tied to your thoughts.

How does observing the dream without becoming involved in it work? For example, you might become lucid in a stressful dream. Becoming lucid in a stressful dream is one of life's greatest joys, and there are infinite ways for the dreamer to behave once lucid. She could yell at her boss who, in reality, is a source of strife in her life. Or she may fly away, through the windows of the building, off to have some adventure. Particularly in a stressful dream, it may be tempting to escape the scene once lucid. Remember, though, that you need not move your physical body in order to explore the dream world. The dream state is perceptually unstable, and if you pause for a long time to observe it, you will notice it changing without your conscious effort to change it.

One way for us to increase our understanding of individual differences in dreaming is for lucid dreamers to mindfully observe their dreams as they are without interfering, and to return to the waking world with detailed reports of what unfolded. By using your lucid dreams to observe your dreaming mind, you can discover how *your* dream world works and compare this to reports from others.

I am not the only writer and lucid dreaming practitioner who recommends an observant approach to lucid dreaming. Lee Irwin writes, "The goal is to sustain awareness or heightened lucidity of what occurs in the dream rather than to direct the dream to a preconceived or rationalized outcome."[3] He goes on to argue for the importance of paying attention in lucid dreams rather than trying to exert control over the dream environment. He argues that lucid dreamers who pay attention in this way become more aware of the reality of dreams than those who do not do so. He compares this increased understanding to the way that a musical expert is able to hear the chord changes and other details of a song whereas the majority of people will just hear the overall musical impression of the song. You are welcome to passively listen to the music of your dreams, but with lucid dreaming, you can listen in order to understand how the music truly operates.

Drugs

Within the dream world you have the ability to draw up anything you have experienced in waking life and experience it again with considerable accuracy to the original experience. If you have taken a particular drug, you can do so in a dream and feel similar effects even in the absence of an external cause.

As David Jay Brown observes in *Dreaming Wide Awake*, "'Dream psychedelics can be used within lucid dreams that have genuine psychological effects." Terence McKenna used to smoke DMT in his lucid dreams, and observed, "You only have to convince your brain that you have done this [smoked DMT] and it then delivers this staggering altered state."[4]

I would recommend that addicts in recovery, who might be triggered by this experience, proceed with extreme caution and guidance. Non-lucid dreams of drug use happen to addicts in recovery. That cannot be helped. An addict may wake up extremely relieved to find that the dream was not real. Lucid dreaming could be a path to even greater healing for addicts in recovery, if they are able to harness lucidity in order to learn more about their own psychology and utilize dreams as a newfound source of joy. I am not sure if using drugs you have quit in the dream state would have a positive, negative, or neutral effect on cravings for those drugs in your waking life. I would not recommend using drugs in a lucid dream without first consulting a professional psychologist.

That said, if you have a healthy relationship with a particular substance and you wish to re-create the feeling of being on that drug in the dream state, you certainly can do so. Remember that, in order to smoke marijuana in a dream, for example, you do not need physical objects such as a joint or a lighter. You can merely conjure up the *feeling* of being high, and, likely, your brain will respond in kind with an intimation of that experience.

It is always important to keep neurodiversity in mind when discussing lucid dreaming. Neurodiversity, the fact that there is considerable variation in how the human brain operates from individual to individual, is part of the reason why I try not to generalize about dreaming. I make no claim that *everyone* can learn how to lucid dream any more than I would claim that *everyone* can learn how to meditate. These skills take considerable effort, and likely require different levels of effort, depending on an individual's mind and personality.

Neurodiversity seems like a particularly apt topic under the subheading of dreamed drug experiences. It is hard to say with certainty how much variation occurs in dream perception. Scientists can measure and compare easily quantifiable factors, such as whether individuals dream in color or black and white, what kind of perspective they have in their dreams, and so forth. But much about the dream experience exists in the realm beyond easily quantifiable concepts. The impossibility of third-party observation makes it difficult to determine with certainty how much our dreams vary. We can never directly compare our own dreams to anyone else's.

In a similar manner, when it comes to drug experiences, we mainly have our words to go by. In a lab setting, a scientific observer could measure biological responses to substance ingestion, such as pupil dilation and heart rate, and even psychological factors such as the individual's mood as reported by that individual. Most people, however, do not usually take recreational drugs in a lab setting. We know simply from speaking to one another that two or more people taking the same dosage of the same substance can have wildly different experiences.

It stands to reason, then, that if you combine two highly subjective and variable mind states, intoxication and dream, there may be considerable variation in individual experiences. For that reason, I do not wish to make any general arguments about the use of drugs in a lucid dream, other than to tell you that it is possible. Hopefully, as lucid dreaming increases in popularity, more data will arise to help us compare subjective, individual experiences of taking various drugs in a lucid dream. Most importantly, researchers should investigate the impact that such experiences could have on an individual in recovery from drug addiction. In general, there is not enough current research on the clinical, therapeutic uses of lucid dreaming for individuals with various mental health conditions.

Final Advice

You are always welcome to approach your lucid dreams spontaneously, but if you are interested in specific activities such as flying or eating chocolate cake, for example, attempt these tasks one at a time. I recommend beginning with whatever seems like it will be the easiest task you want to try, and build from there.

Given the importance of your own confidence and expectations in determining your level of dream control, it is best not to try too much too soon in your lucid dreams, as this can lead to you becoming discouraged and building up mental blocks against your own success. If you find it incredibly easy to locate and eat a delicious piece of cake in your dream, you will go into your next lucid dream with increased confidence, and have an easier time achieving the next task you have set out to achieve.

In my own experience, talking to dream characters may be the easiest activity mentioned in this chapter. Observing is also fairly simple. Exploring and flying are moderately difficult. Having sex, practicing a sport or instrument, making objects appear, and changing the scenery are all challenging activities. You may want to put them off until you have more practice with simpler tasks. Meditation and drug use are hard to quantify in terms of difficulty, as they depend considerably on your waking life experience. An experienced meditator may have little difficulty meditating in a dream, whereas a new meditator may struggle considerably.

You most likely have a good idea, even before trying any of these activities, which you will struggle with the most. Use your instincts and start small. Once you have identified a particular activity to try, you may want to incubate that dream with the techniques outlined in the following section.

ACTIVITY GOALS

1. Write a list of all lucid dreaming activities you would like to try.
2. Order these from easiest to most challenging.
3. Incorporate these into your short-term and long-term lucid dreaming goals.
4. Assess your progress at the end of each month in your dream journal.

Dream Incubation

Dream incubation is a technique that can help you to successfully achieve any of the aforementioned activities. This technique dates back to ancient Egypt, and has been utilized by individuals to induce a dream with a particular kind of content. Dream incubation can be used for both lucid and non-lucid dreams.

Through dream incubation, you can decide not only that you want to have a lucid dream or try a particular activity, but you can further influence the content of the dream from the outset. Thus, instead of deciding you want to have a lucid dream in which you find and speak to a particular person, you could incubate a dream about that person and remember to use their presence to trigger a reality check.

One way that you can incubate a dream with particular content is to focus not necessarily on achieving lucidity, but instead to focus on your intention to have a dream with the particular content. So, for example, if you want to have a lucid dream which takes place in the woods, then before bed, use visualization and autosuggestion techniques to influence your mind to produce a dream which takes place in the woods. Lucidity, in this case, can be secondary. Focus on your intention to have a dream in the woods. Also remember to use the forest scenery as a trigger for your lucidity. Thus, incubating a dream with particular content can in itself be a technique for achieving lucidity, or it can simply be a technique for influencing your dreams. You might not even necessarily want to incubate a *lucid* dream. You might simply want to utilize your waking imagination to influence the content of your dreams.

Dream incubation techniques are commonly used for creative problem solving. Let's say you are working on a difficult math problem or trying to figure out what the main character in your novel should do next. You can have a lucid dream in which you ponder the problem directly, using the uniquely creative mind state of dreaming. Or you can incubate a dream (again, lucid or not) to help you work on this problem. Your creative, dreaming mind may provide the answer directly, but more likely it will provide you with an indirect response.

For example, if you have worked on your problem for a few hours, you may wish to take a nap and have a dream that is in some way related to the problem. Try to visualize yourself in a dream working on the problem. Use autosuggestion to influence your mind, thinking or saying phrases like *This dream will guide me to my answer*. Remember that the clues your dreaming mind provides might not be completely direct. Set aside time to journal after you awaken in order to parse apart your dreaming mind's answer to your waking mind's question.

Dream incubation as a concept is very similar to other lucid dreaming techniques and can be used with them. These techniques will be most effective at a time closer to REM sleep. Thus, you could try these techniques before bed, but it may be more effective to combine dream incubation with the Wake Back to Bed method. To do this, remember to set an alarm six hours into sleep. When you wake up, visualize the subject or setting you want to dream about. You can sketch the dream out or write about it as well. As you fall back asleep, stay focused on your intention. As you can see, this process is almost identical to attempting a wake-induced lucid dream, except that it is focused on the content of the dream rather than on achieving lucidity.

I have not personally experimented very much with dream incubation, as I prefer to observe my dreams as they are and not interfere too much with their natural content. However, I did accidentally incubate a particular dream once. I had set an activity goal to try meditating in my next lucid dream. Instead of having a lucid dream and remembering to meditate, however, I ended up having a non-lucid dream that took place in a meditation hall. Here are my notes from the dream:

I find myself in a meditation center, which reminds me of the plan I had made to meditate in a dream. I realize that I'm dreaming. I sit down on one of the bright green meditation cushions, to meditate. Out of the window I can see that the sky looks gorgeous, full of swirling purple clouds. The cars and people outside all look very surreal to me. Other people begin to fill the room and we meditate together.

By setting an intention and focusing on it in my waking life, I had induced a dream about meditation. As soon as I noticed my surroundings, I became lucid. This serves to demonstrate how our waking minds can influence our dreaming minds in countless ways.

10

Long-Term Goal Setting

*I*n the section on keeping a dream journal, I suggested that readers set goals for their lucid dreaming practice, such as identifying a number of lucid dreams to have per month. The goals I outlined in that chapter are short-term goals. Making long-term goals will help you to identify what it is you want to gain from a prolonged lucid dreaming practice, and think about the big picture of how lucid dreaming should fit into your life and lifestyle.

Setting these types of goals will put you in a position to evaluate how you are doing six months or a year in the future. Long-term goals can help you to stick with your lucid dreaming practice even through small setbacks or disappointments. It takes a good deal of intrinsic motivation to retain the habits of dream journaling, reality checking, dream analysis, and dream incubation practices over the long term.

I do not want to dismiss any particular goals, no matter how seemingly trivial. In *The Tibetan Yogas of Dream and Sleep*, Rinpoche argues that it does not actually matter what we do in our lucid dreams, so long as the activities we engage in teach us about the fleeting nature of form. In his view, learning to fly, or to change the appearance of objects, is no more or less important than seeking spiritual guidance or meditating in a dream would be.

That said, this practice is what you make of it, and your relationship with lucid dreaming will likely change as you grow and change as a person. When I first began lucid dreaming as a young child, my pursuits were a child's pursuits. My favorite lucid dreaming activity was to show off. I often had dreams that took place in a school environment, among my friends, and I loved to show my friends what I could do. I felt like I had magical powers. This was an immensely pleasurable and enjoyable activity at the time, but it no longer brings me the same joy as an adult. I have grown into a person with different goals and my lucid dreaming practice reflects that.

The activity goals I have asked you to identify for yourself are most likely to be long-term goals (unless you achieve them all effortlessly). As you become proficient in a particular activity, you may grow out of it. Or, as you change as a person overall in your life, your pursuits may change. No matter what your content-based goals currently are, it is a good idea to solidify them in your mind in order to set yourself up to be able to track your progress.

At the beginning of the month, write down what skills you are currently working towards cultivating. Writing those skills down will help you to remember to try these activities in a lucid dream. At the end of the month, take the time to reflect on whether you remembered to try these activities in your dreams and whether or not they worked as planned. If you were incapable of executing a particular activity, reflect on why this was. Did doubt impact your confidence? If so, try visualization techniques for improving your belief in yourself. Were you too distracted by emotions, thoughts, or the dream plot? Try meditating before bed next time you want to have a lucid dream.

For years now, every month, I have set and evaluated my lucid dreaming goals. It is easy to remember to track my lucid dreams and other goals at the end of every month. One month often feels like enough time to achieve a goal, such as trying to meditate in a lucid dream. If I gave myself longer than one month, it might take the pressure off so much so that I forget about my goal and don't put enough effort into achieving it. Expecting myself to try a new lucid dream activity in the span of a week or two, however, does not feel like enough time.

Beyond the ever-changing, content-based goals you form for your lucid dreams, you likely have broader goals for how you want to use lucidity to guide your waking life. You might be hoping for lucid dreams to provide you with ideas or inspiration for problem solving or artwork. You might be hoping for lucid dreaming to weave into your mindfulness meditation practice, allowing you to cultivate awareness continuously throughout your waking and your dreaming life. Whatever these goals may be, approach them the same way you approach your activity goals. Solidify your intentions by writing them down. Track them at some predetermined future date. Make goal setting an integral part of your dream journaling process.

One way you might want to use lucid dreaming to improve your waking life is simply by increasing your dream recall and analyzing the dreams in your dream journal for purposes of psychological growth. Thus far, I have discussed dream analysis exclusively as a means of achieving lucid dreams. Of course, you can also analyze the meaning of your dreams in order to gain a greater understanding of your own emotions and to make decisions in your waking life. The next section will discuss this kind of psychological dream analysis.

Dream Analysis

There are countless reasons why you might want to analyze the contents of your dream journal. If you are feeling stuck or unsure in your life, if your waking mind isn't providing any new ideas or answers to long-standing problems, it is at those times that I most recommend turning to your dreams for creative insight.

Unfortunately, people in modern American society rarely discuss their dreams with anyone other than close friends and romantic partners, and even then they tend to do so only when they remember a particularly striking dream. Given that nearly 30 percent of American adults sleep for six hours or less a night, compared to less than 2 percent of Americans who were sleep deprived 100 years ago,[1] we are less likely than ever before to *remember* our dreams, let alone value, share, and analyze them.

In contrast, in other geographic locations, cultures, and time periods, human beings have demonstrated profound respect for their dreams and incorporated dream analysis into their lives in various practical and spiritual ways. I have spoken throughout this book of the Tibetan traditions of sleep and dream yoga. The Tibetans are by no means the only people who have historically integrated dreams into waking life. Indigenous peoples of Australia, and First Nations Iroquois, have historically begun their days by sharing their dreams with one another. The content of their dreams provided them with individual insight, and dreams were also considered important guiding tools for the entire community.

10. Long-Term Goal Setting

In the Talmud, the major text of Rabbinic Judaism, Rav Hisda states, "An uninterpreted dream is like an unopened letter" (Talmud Bavli, Brachot 55a). Dreams contain information, whether we choose to engage with that information or not. In Greece, Artemidorus wrote his five-book *Oneirocritica*, the first extant book on the subject of dream interpretation, in the second century AD. For thousands of years, people have wondered about the meaning of their dreams.

Your views on dream interpretation are likely influenced by your cultural background. As a child and teenager, I sought out books about lucid dreaming. In bookstores and libraries, I could not find any such books. Instead, I found only books about sleep and dreams, especially dream interpretation books that were simple dictionaries of symbols. This did not sit well with me, as I believe that symbols are personal. While there are overarching symbolic ideas among specific cultures and even among human beings as a whole, a mountain is not for me what a mountain is for you. We each have our own experiences and associations.

Writing his *Oneirocritica* 1,800 years ago, Artemidorus argued much the same thing. While his book did contain a dictionary of overarching symbols, he also argued for the importance of understanding the dreamer in order to interpret her dream. He believed that images in the dream function largely as metaphors that need to be deciphered, and he believed that the individual dreamer's waking life experiences have an impact on her dream symbology.

Freud's theory on dream interpretation, arguably the most well-known dream analysis theory to date, relied heavily on the concept of symbolism. In fact, he believed that our dreams revealed our unconscious desires, but that interpretation was necessary to uncover these taboo wishes. For that reason, he differentiated between what he termed the "manifest content" and "latent content" of dreams. Freud's manifest content is equivalent to what I call the dream plot: it is the evident action of the dream. According to Freud, the manifest content must be analyzed to uncover the true meaning of the dream, its latent content. He also coined the term "censoring agency" to describe the mechanism of transformation that turns our unconscious wishes into the manifest content of our dreams. In Freud's view, dreams are a way for us to process the desires that we are too ashamed to admit to ourselves, let alone to others.

Section Two—Why Learn to Lucid Dream?

Since Freud, there have been dozens of other, notable dream theorists. Carl Jung is another well-known dream theorist. Jung was good friends with Freud until they had a falling out, due in large part to their disagreement over dream analysis. While he believed that dreams could involve symbolism, he did not agree with Freud's concept of a censoring agency. Jung's opinion on dream symbolism is more in line with Artemidorus than with Freud. Bulkeley writes, Jung "says there are no fixed meanings to any symbols—all dream symbols must be related to the dreamer's unique waking-life situation. But on the other hand, he believes that dreams regularly contain archetypal symbols, whose meanings are universal, transcending the dreamer's individual consciousness."[2] Jung further argued that dreams can provide prospective visions of future events.

I tend to agree with Jung and with Artemidorus. In my experience, dream symbols are highly personal, revealing meaning to the dreamer which would not be interpreted universally by others. At the same time, there are, curiously, a number of dream images that emerge over and over again. So many people have dreams of flying, being naked in public, and watching their teeth fall out of their mouths, that we might well ask ourselves if there are universal meanings to such images. Take the example of teeth falling out. This is almost universally an unpleasant dream experience, accompanied by the emotion of distress. I'm not sure why so many people experience this exact dream image, but I would imagine that this falls under the general category of a "stress dream," most likely occurring in times of high stress. You might ask yourself, if you have this dream, what kind of stressor in your waking life has triggered it, which is of course an individual matter. Thus, even universal dream symbols bring us back to the personal.

You are not alone if you believe dream interpretation to be a personal, individualistic process. Beyond the meaning of specific symbols, it is up to the individual to decide whether her dreams are meaningful and in what way. In order to consider the role of dream analysis, the act of discovering meaning within the dream realm, we have to individually reflect on our own definition of meaning. In other words: what does *meaning* mean? Attempting to define "meaning" is an aggravatingly recursive process. But if you cannot articulate what *meaning* is, how will you know whether a dream of yours is meaningful, and in what way? This is why the process of analyzing your dreams is typically referred to as dream "interpretation." An individual cannot decode or read your dream's meaning for you; this meaning must be *interpreted*, and that interpretation is bound to be subjective.

Rinpoche mirrors this sentiment. He states that "the meaning of a book, like a dream, is subject to interpretation. Two people can read the same book and have entirely different experiences; one person may change her whole life based on the meaning she has found in the pages, while her friend may find the book only mildly interesting or not even that. The book has not changed. The meaning is projected onto the words by the reader, and then read back."[3] Thus, like a book or a letter, you have the choice of leaving your dreams unopened, unread. You also have the choice of reading your dreams more for entertainment than for insight. The extent to which your dreams reveal information to you has a good deal to do with your personality.

It is for that reason that I've included cursory descriptions of major dream analysis theories, so that you can ask yourself which theory holds the most potential usefulness for you. Freud and Jung are perhaps the most well known, but by no means the only, theorists. In the 1930s, Frederick Perls combined ideas from psychoanalysis, existentialism, and Gestalt psychology into his own theory of dream analysis. He used a therapeutic approach, asking dreamers to embody each visual element of the dream. For example, if you dreamt of a car crash over a cliff with your friend, Perls would ask you to describe that dream from your own perspective as well as the perspective of the car, the cliff, and the friend. He also argued that it is necessary to do so while speaking in the present tense. It is perhaps for this reason that some lucid dreaming books recommend writing your dream journal in the present tense.

American psychologist Calvin Hall used a different approach than others mentioned in this chapter. He created a methodology for quantitatively analyzing dreams. He drew upon dream reports, sorting the content into the categories of characters, social interactions, emotions, settings, and objects. These were then converted into numbers, allowing Hall to statistically analyze large numbers of dreams from several dreamers, as well as to analyze patterns in an individual's dreams over time. He strongly disagreed with Freud's theory, arguing, "The images of a dream are the concrete embodiments of the dreamer's thoughts; these images give visible expression to that which is invisible, namely, conceptions. Accordingly the true referent of any dream symbol is not an object or activity, it is always an idea in the mind of the dreamer."[4]

When I speak of the important role which expectations play in dreams, I am mirroring Hall's statement. Expectations are thoughts. In dreams, thoughts manifest visually. Thus, I agree with Hall's statement that dreamed objects result from thoughts. Thus, I suppose, dream images are meaningful in the same sense and to the same extent that our thoughts are meaningful. David Foulkes makes a similar argument, saying that "dreaming is generated by the same cognitive systems that produce ordinary speech in waking life. Dreams do not speak in a 'special language'; they speak in the same basic language, following the same basic grammatical rules, that we use when we are awake."[5] Thoughts often occur as language. Therefore, Hall, Foulkes, and I make a similar argument: that our thoughts, in the form of language, directly create dream images and events.

Harry Hunt, a psychologist at Brock University, created his own classification system for dreams. He believed that dreams can be sorted into six major categories. Personal-mnemonic dreams concern everyday matters. Medical-somatic dreams relate to the dreamer's body and health. Prophetic dreams predict events in the future which may occur. Archetypal-spiritual dreams involve vivid encounters with symbolic or universally transcendent beings. The final two categories—nightmares and lucid dreams—are discussed at length in this book. Hunt dismissed any generalized theory about the main purpose or function of dreams, arguing instead that there are likely countless purposes for dreaming and we need not identify a single overarching one.

Clara Hill, a psychology professor at the University of Maryland, is leading a resurgence of dream work in therapy. She recommends that therapists ask their clients what they would change about a given dream's content, which opens up discussions about changes they would like to make in their waking lives as well.

Whatever your perspective on dream analysis may be, there is an undeniable connection between our waking concerns and the content of our dreams. I only discovered the potential usefulness of dream analysis several years after I began dream journaling. Personally, I have found that dreams provide useful information to me which I could not have discovered in any other way. The information that I tend to "hide" from my waking self, so to speak, is chiefly concerned with emotions. In other words, I do not always know or admit to myself how I am *feeling*, but this information often comes through clearly in the dream realm. Perhaps, unlike me, you have no trouble knowing how you are feeling. Perhaps other information comes through your dreaming mind, helping you solve problems, make difficult decisions, or make connections between seemingly disparate aspects of your knowledge.

The one most significant dream interpretation experience I had occurred spontaneously. I was not looking for guidance in my life. I was looking, instead, for dreamsigns. I decided to read through my dream entries from the previous two months, in order to inform myself about the content of my dreams. I did so with the goal of increasing my lucid dreams. Instead, what I found was strikingly obvious symbolic dream content, which revealed to me emotions that I had kept hidden from myself.

For months, I had been mildly concerned about my relationship, but I did not let this dominate my consciousness. Something seemed off between me and my partner, but I could not pinpoint anything specific that had gone wrong. I thought that I was being anxious and paranoid, and therefore felt better off putting my worries out of my mind. I was not successful, however, in pushing the feelings away. They emerged through my dreams. While I consistently kept a daily dream journal at this time, I only did so as an automatic habit for the purpose of maintaining dream recall. I did not pay careful attention to my dreams as I wrote them down.

Reading through the previous two months of entries, I found dream after dream about being left behind, forgotten, abandoned. In one particular dream, I found myself with my partner and some mutual friends. We were headed on a grand adventure in my partner's car. Outside of the car, though, we got separated, and I watched them drive off without me. Practically all of my dreams had followed a similar formula. I simply hadn't noticed as I wrote them down.

Reading through my dream journal it was suddenly clear that I had been experiencing strong anxiety about the fear of being left by my partner and also losing friends in the process. The feelings I had tried not to feel were still being felt, only in sleep. By the time that I realized this, my partner had indeed decided to leave me. The very thing I had subconsciously feared would happen, had happened; thus my dreams in hindsight felt almost prophetic. Of course, in this case, they were not prophetic. I felt my partner distance himself from me, and I had refused to consciously acknowledge this, while my unconscious mind tried to do the processing for me.

If I had paid closer attention to my dreams as I recorded them, perhaps I would have confronted my own emotions and let myself feel them rather than trying to snuff them out. This could have led to a quicker or more complete emotional healing process for me during and after the breakup. It is rather difficult to say. If you are feeling unsure about your own emotions, or having trouble making a particular decision, you may want to read through your dream journal with an open mind. You do not need to be on the lookout for anything. If you have a few weeks' or months' worth of dreams to read through, patterns in your thinking will emerge. Whether you find the content meaningful and what you do with the information is up to you and your personal definition of "meaningful."

In my experience, patterns simply jump out to me with obvious, personal meaning. I do not consider myself visually symbolic in how I think, thus I do not necessarily hunt for the "hidden" meaning behind dream content. In my example, I dreamt of being literally left behind and experiencing anxiety as a result. The connection to my waking life was obvious.

In high school I used to have anxious dreams wherein I found myself smoking cigarettes. I dreamt of smoking more often than I actually smoked. A friend of mine joked, drawing upon a Freudian perspective, that the symbol was "obviously phallic." I knew that in fact I was trying to work through my anxiety, fear, and guilt over having an unhealthy habit of which I knew others in my life would disapprove. Thus, the cigarette didn't symbolize some hidden meaning. Cigarettes symbolized cigarettes.

You, however, might be someone whose brain works very differently than mine does. For you, dream images might clearly be symbolic of something which I would never be able to interpret for you. In short, your dreams mean whatever you think they mean. Use your instincts. Dreams come from your own brain and only your own brain can interpret them accurately.

The above examples serve to illustrate the individual nature of dream interpretation, and how looking up an image in a dream symbol dictionary is not enough to tell you what your dreams mean. You have to put your dreams in the context of your waking life's circumstances, your own thought process, and your personality. Given the fact that dreams are a product of our own mind, it stands to reason that sifting through your dream journal will offer added insight into the inner workings of your psyche. While others may assist you in interpretation, you alone can ultimately determine what, if anything, your dreams mean to you.

11

Dreaming's Influence on Creativity and Invention

*F*rom the sewing machine, to the melody of the Beatles' "Yesterday," to Mary Shelley's *Frankenstein*, to Kekulé's proof of the circular structure of molecules—countless creative and scientific feats have been achieved in the dream state, or shortly upon waking from a dream. Given that dreams can spontaneously provide us with answers to difficult problems, or creative ideas for the arts, lucid dreaming offers a world of possibilities for intentionally utilizing the dream space.

Creativity

In the chapter "Common Mistakes," I relayed a scene from the 1920s surrealist novel *The Third Policeman,* in which the main character finds himself in a magical place where he can conjure any object at will, but discovers that he cannot take any of those objects back to reality with him. Even beyond the realm of physical objects, you may find yourself in a *Third Policeman*–esque predicament when it comes to bringing ideas back to the waking world with you.

I have roughly twenty years of experience with lucid dreams. As a creative person, I have spent many dreams conjuring story ideas, songs, scripts, visual art and more. Occasionally I have an idea in a lucid dream which feels so brilliant to me at the time that I spend the rest of the dream trying desperately to hold the melody or the line of dialogue in my conscious mind until I wake up.

These creative lucid dreams in which I decide I want to bring an idea back to the waking realm ultimately go one of three ways. I may wake up and, in spite of all my efforts, forget the idea. This is doubly frustrating because I feel that I have lost the idea and wasted the lucid dream. I may wake up remembering the idea but find that my waking self does not find it brilliant at all. Instead, I find it incomprehensible. This is most true with story ideas, but even melodies have occasionally lost their brilliance for me upon waking. In the third case I may successfully bring the idea back and use it in some form. This third case, unfortunately, is extremely rare for me. I usually either forget the idea or decide that it was not actually worthwhile.

If you are skilled at waking yourself up, you may want to utilize this technique to bring an idea to your waking world, where you can jot it down. Do remember, though, the possibility that your sleeping mind and your waking mind have different opinions on what constitutes a brilliant idea.

Dreams are an innately meaning-infused state of mind. Lucid dreams especially seem to press a "meaningful" button in the human brain. Once you realize that everything outside of you is a figment of your imagination, this vastly changes the way you see and consider all that you are perceiving. Along with the dissolution of boundaries and the expansion of possibilities comes an innate feeling—a feeling of the *importance* of the experience. Perhaps Rinpoche is correct when he asserts that it does not matter what precisely you do in your lucid dreams, so long as the actions you perform dissolve boundaries and thus teach you about the underlying nature of reality. Perhaps lucid dreams teach us about the true nature of reality. Perhaps we also, on some level, know this, and thus lucid dreams feel innately meaningful regardless of what we do in them, because they teach us something true and important.

Keep in mind that nearly everything in the lucid dream might feel meaningful to you in the moment. The experience of being in a highly convincing hallucination, which you are partly directing with your mind, while understanding that it is all a figment of your imagination—this is an awe-inspiring experience, even if you've had it hundreds or thousands of times. It feels inherently meaningful. Just as Marshall McLuhan argued that, in the real of media, "the medium is the message," perhaps "the mind state is the message." In other words, perhaps the dream state itself is what feels meaningful, not the content of particular dream ideas. You may feel like you have to bring everything back with you. But perhaps you don't. Perhaps merely experiencing that meaning-infused state will have a positive impact on your waking creativity, without any further effort on your part.

This philosophical aside points to a real, practical question as far as using lucid dreams for creative purposes is concerned. How *precisely* should we "use" lucid dreams for creative purposes? Should the dreams serve primarily as a meaning-rife source of inspiration, or should we use the lucid dream as a space and time to engage in creative acts such as painting, playing music, or thinking of ideas for narratives?

The answer can, of course, be both, and ultimately the connection between dreams and creativity is not likely to be linear. We may have one particular dream in which we write a melody, or conjure up a new character for a story, intentionally or unintentionally, but the overall impact of dreams on creativity is impossible to measure in a clear way. For that reason, learning how to lucid dream may have an impact on your creative, problem-solving pursuits which may not be easy to pinpoint, but may be intrinsically felt.

That said, let's move on to some specifics of how the state can be utilized. I tend to mostly think of creative dream pursuits as a form of play—enjoyable for their own sake. While I believe that this type of play likely enhances my creative abilities overall, I do not tend to focus anymore on bringing anything back with me. It takes an intense amount of focus to bring dream ideas back to the waking world. Consider, for example, that it may be the middle of the night, with multiple rounds of REM sleep and countless dreams still ahead of you. It is hard enough to remember *anything* from a dream, let alone bring back four bars of a melody.

I may sound like a hypocrite, as elsewhere in this book I have argued for the importance of bringing certain types of data back from the dream world with you. Specifically, I have urged readers to learn as much as they can about the dream state and how it functions, and to bring that information back to the waking world in order to inform your understanding of reality and your mind. That is a rather different action, though, than repeating a specific melody over and over in the hopes of remembering it. Focusing your attention on the dream state itself is a relaxed activity. You are not interfering, just observing. You do not need to focus on remembering anything in particular. This is an experiential type of learning, in which you bring back your general impressions, which you gained through passive experience. You can do this countless times.

That is not to say that you will not create breathtaking artwork in your dreams, or utilize them to solve problems. Creating artwork is likely among the most fulfilling lucid dream activities you will try. You can use your dreams as a time and space for creating, and that space will be awe-inspiringly open-ended. You don't even need a paintbrush; you can paint with your mind! Of course, the catch is, you can't take it with you.

Perhaps your experiences of creating artwork in the dream will provide a direct inspiration for a piece of art you will create when you wake. Or perhaps the boundary-dissolving experience of lucid dreaming itself, more generally, will influence your work. Artists draw upon experiences from all areas of their lives in order to create. Becoming increasingly aware in your dreams and remembering more of your dreams will provide you with an entirely new area of experience from which to draw inspiration and content for your art.

I will conclude with an example of a brief moment in a non-lucid dream wherein my waking thoughts about creativity influenced my dreamed thoughts. In this dream I was able to take back an image with me, which, while I will probably not use the specific image itself, reflected my intention to view the world through a more creative lens:

> *I'm driving at the end of my street. I notice the sun casting a shadow diagonally across the red, graffiti-covered fence. I think about how this is the sort of detail I should include in my fiction, and I'm pleased to notice the act of writing affecting my thoughts in this way.*

Problem Solving and Invention

Elias Howe invented the sewing machine with the help of a dream. He knew that the sewing machine would involve a needle and cloth, but did not know exactly how the parts would function together. At the time in his life when he was pondering this problem, he had a dream in which he was being attacked by people with spears, and he noticed that their spears had holes in them, near the point of the spear. When he awoke, his dream still in his mind, he realized that he could put a hole in the needle nearer to the point, a crucial factor which allows sewing machines to function.

Note that he did not dream about a functional sewing machine. If he had forgotten or not taken adequate note of his dream content, he may not have solved the problem at hand. He could have easily dismissed his dream as a useless nightmare. Thus, if you decide to "sleep on" a problem in your life, remember to write down your dreams when you wake up. Do not expect an answer to come to you in clear, easy-to-understand terms. If the dream content does not seem to provide any clues to your problem, it is still a good idea to return to your work upon waking, with your mind refreshed.

New ideas for how to solve your problem may emerge without a clear connection to the dream. A good night's sleep is essential to the act of problem solving. Even if you can't draw a clear connection from your dreams to your waking ideas, there is a connection, and there is likely to be an even greater connection if you utilize dream incubation to guide your subconscious mind. While it may at first seem frustrating that the answers your dreams provide are not straightforward, the fact that the process is somewhat mysterious and nonlinear makes dreams that much more magical.

12

Meditation

*E*xperienced meditators and lucid dreamers will not be surprised to discover that there has been research demonstrating strong connections between the two states on a neurological level. Researchers have found that the same EEG patterns occur "during focused wake, default wake, meditation, and lucid dreaming states—all teachable states of focused awareness under conscious control, with similarities in reported effects on cognitive processing, attention, and recall."[1] There is also a historical and cultural connection between lucid dreaming and meditation, as both practices have ties to Buddhist spiritual traditions and are in fact interwoven into certain practices. The Tibetan practice of sleep and dream yoga involves both meditation and lucid dreaming techniques. What's more, frequent meditators report significantly more lucid dreams than non-meditators do.[2]

In the chapter "Common Mistakes," I argued for the importance of not only remembering to perform reality checks, but also being willing to stop yourself in the midst of even the strongest emotional turmoil. This is a tall order indeed. What I am asking you to do is to stop dead in your tracks, precisely when it feels the least practical for you to do so. Anything and everything you most care about may appear to be on the line: your friends, your family, your own personal safety, your job, your possessions, your finances, your reputation. Lucid dreaming helps to teach us how often these fears are not real, as well as the importance and potential in realizing the unreality of your imagined fears.

Meditators will know the difficulty of stopping their thought stream and emotional turmoil all too well. Remembering to stop and perform a reality check in the middle of emotional distress is analogous to the act of remembering to draw attention to the present moment throughout your day as a mindfulness practice.

If you are currently a meditator, you may be looking for ways to weave your mindfulness practice and your lucid dreaming practice together. If you rarely or never meditate, you may want to consider at least occasionally meditating, given the similarities between lucid dreaming and meditation.

To begin with, though, I need to define mindfulness and meditation more specifically. Jon Kabat-Zinn, the founder of Mindfulness-Based Stress Reduction, defines mindfulness as "awareness that arises through paying attention, on purpose, in the present moment, non-judgmentally."[3] Meditation is a concentrated and intentional mindfulness practice, which takes many forms, but often involves drawing attention to something specific such as the breath, body sensations, sounds, or to a particular visualized image or external object.

As you have learned, lucid dreaming similarly involves paying careful attention, on purpose, to the present moment. Specifically, a lucid dreaming practice requires you to bring a certain kind of attention to the present moment, in asking yourself whether you are awake or asleep at any given time. You may find that, without even meaning to, you are experiencing a more mindful and meditative perspective on life simply through practicing daily reality checks, since reality checks ask you to increase your present-moment awareness throughout the day.

This book is primarily about lucid dreaming and will not give you an in-depth understanding of meditation, but in this chapter, I provide some basic information needed to try a simple meditation practice. During meditation, thoughts will occur. You do not need to "try not to think." That is a common misconception held about meditation.

Let's say you are engaging in a five-minute meditation during which you are attempting to hold your attention on your breath. After a few mindful breaths, thoughts will emerge. Just notice your thoughts as they come, and whenever you remember, return your attention to your breath. Sound simple? It is simple. Outside of a fixed period of meditation, people seeking greater awareness in their lives then strive to draw their attention to the present moment and to their breathing throughout the day. Thus, meditation serves as a concentrated time to practice what you are striving to achieve as an overall state of mind. Meditation is the practice, while mindfulness is the overarching goal.

I have meditated on and off for the past decade, but I have much more experience as a lucid dreamer than I do as a meditator. That said, I have enough experience with meditation that I can draw strong connections between meditation and lucid dreaming. A common experience that I have, which I'm sure other practitioners of meditation can relate to, is that I remember to draw my attention to my breath, but at the same time I experience a strong resistance to actually doing so.

My level of resistance towards my own awareness, my resistance towards the present moment, is proportional to the level and kind of emotion I am experiencing in that particular moment. For example, let's say I am in a fairly good mood. My mind may wander in a daydreaming sort of way but I am not fixating on any particular worries about the future or regrets about my past. Then, when I remember to draw my attention to the breath and the present moment, I feel no resistance to doing so. I have no trouble interrupting my stream of thought since I recognize that stream of thought as unimportant, or at least less important than the cultivation of present-moment awareness.

Now, compare this with another moment later in the day. Perhaps I'm out with friends in a beautiful forest, having a pleasant walk, but my mind has drifted to some financial worries. I start calculating my bills and income for the month, doing the math in my head. My thoughts are fixated on a specific problem, my financial situation, and at the same time that problem is imbued with strong negative emotions of stress. In this moment, if I remember to draw my attention to the breath, I will feel a strong resistance to doing so. While I can recognize the present moment as important, and worth experiencing, my thoughts about my finances feel a good deal more important. These thoughts feel important chiefly because they are imbued with a strong, and negative, emotional content. I feel I need to *fix* this problem.

We must constantly remind ourselves that a great deal of life's problems cannot be fixed through thought alone. Instead, incessant thinking robs us of precious moments. Reality is ripped away in favor of fantasy, especially if the fantasy is an emotional one. Personally, I find that negative emotions are particularly resistant to the act of awareness. You may similarly find a particular emotion to be more of a distraction to you than others.

If you wish to use mindfulness to enhance your lucid dreaming practice, try to practice present-moment awareness throughout your waking as well as your dreaming life. Take note of when you find it most difficult to do so. Are you experiencing a strong emotion? Is it positive or negative? Are there one or two emotions that are particularly hard to disengage with? Take note of these in your dream journal. Let's say, for example, that you have a particularly hard time returning attention to your breath, or conducting a reality check, when you are feeling angry about something. Be sure to look out for moments of anger and perform a reality check precisely then, when it is hardest for you to do so.

In both the case of performing a reality check and the case of returning attention to the present moment, you are attempting to stop or pause your stream of thoughts and place your awareness and attention elsewhere: on the reality of this moment. If your thoughts have a strong emotional content, you may not want to notice your breath or ask yourself whether or not you are dreaming. In a dream, dismissing the reality check or being so caught up in thought and emotion that you cannot even remember to perform a reality check has the unfortunate consequence of a missed opportunity for lucidity. This is especially frustrating when you wake up in the morning and realize you spent your dream stressed about worries that were not even real. In your waking life, resistance to the present moment robs you of life itself.

What's more, you are likely to find (especially with practice in both lucid dreaming and meditation) that your waking concerns are just as "unreal" as your dream concerns. How many of your anxious thoughts actually come to fruition? It would be near impossible to pin down an exact percentage of how many fears become realities, but certainly it is easy to recognize that most do not. Particularly if you are on the more anxious end of the spectrum, and you conjure up several fantasies of concern per day, the vast majority of those concerns do not come to pass.

You can utilize the connection between lucid dreaming and meditation in any number of ways, depending on what you are hoping to gain from either practice. I have previously recommended that meditators incorporate reality checks into their meditation practice. This may

12. Meditation

seem like adding a step to an already challenging mental habit, but reality checks serve a similar purpose to mindfulness practices. If you aren't sure whether you are awake or dreaming, then can you really say you are aware and focused on the present moment? Meditation and lucid dreaming strengthen each other and have many similar end goals: added awareness, greater calm, flexibility in problem solving, and so on.

Here is my formula for a combined mindful moment and reality check. Try this throughout the day as often as you can manage to: First, determine whether or not you are dreaming. Then, focus your awareness fully on your next breath. Third, notice where you are. If you are awake, proceed with whatever you are currently doing, now with greater awareness and concentration. If you are sleeping, you may now wish to redirect the course of your dream. Your ability to do so will benefit from pausing to take a mindful breath and notice your surroundings.

13

Teaching Children to Lucid Dream

*F*or a moment, put yourself in the perspective of a small child, some-one about three or four years old. At this age, you are acquiring language. You have begun to categorize the world through your emerging vocabulary and you are learning more and more about the world and how it works every day. You still struggle quite a bit in terms of categorizing things, for example, into the simple categories of "living" and "nonliving." You might, knowing that trees, flowers, grass, small plants, and other beings of the forest are alive, mistakenly assume that rocks are alive as well. This would be understandable, and an adult would correct you. Not having necessarily encountered fake flowers before, upon seeing them for the first time, you will most likely assume they are real until corrected.

When it comes to the television screen, some of what appears on it is to some extent "real" (news). Most of what comes through the television is "fake" (shows and movies). Adults will slowly teach you the difference, particularly when assuring you that scary events in shows and movies are not real.

At the end of every day, your parents try to coax you to sleep, which you do not enjoy. They take you from the fun, stimulating environment of the living room into your bedroom. Maybe they read you a story and tuck you in. Then they turn off the light and you are all alone in darkness (except for, perhaps, a nightlight). You close your eyes and eventually flashes of light appear. Those flashes of light and color give way to more distinct forms, and soon you are in a full-fledged narrative. You wake from a nightmare and a parent comes to comfort you, saying, "It's just a dream. It wasn't real. It didn't really happen." They leave you again in darkness to confront the same fears all over again.

It is understandable that children who are just beginning to categorize stimuli into real or not real would be particularly frightened by nightmares, which they have to slowly learn over time to categorize as "not real." What's more, telling a child that the vivid, real-seeming, and terrifying experience they had was just in their head, is called a "dream" or "nightmare," that no one else experienced the frightening event except for them—these assurances may in fact do little to comfort the child.

Instead, giving the child the tools to recognize the dream as unreal *while it is happening* will do considerably more to stave off nightmares, increase an appreciation for dreaming, and, at the same time, validate the child's experience as important even as you explain that it was not real in the same sense as waking reality.

Given all of the potential benefits to lucid dreaming—increased awareness, decreased nightmares, greater enjoyment of sleep, and increased understanding of your own mind—there is no reason we should not begin learning the techniques of lucid dreaming as children. By teaching your children to lucid dream, you give them the tools they need to successfully deal with their nightmares and become less frightened of sleep. As we have seen, the underlying principle in lucidly dealing with nightmares is to confront your fears rather than try to escape them. This approach clearly has benefits in waking life as well. Teaching your children to face their fears in sleep will increase their confidence in their ability to do so in waking life.

In the earlier section about cautions and caveats, I warned against learning how to lucid dream if you have difficulty determining whether or not you are awake. You can easily determine whether or not your child will face this difficulty by simply asking her to perform a reality check. You need not use the words "reality check." Begin by asking your child if she ever has dreams in which she knows she is dreaming. She may already be lucid dreaming without realizing it! If so, then you likely do not need to worry about her ability to distinguish between waking and sleeping, as she is already doing so in some of her dreams.

If she has never had a lucid dream, you could ask her if she is dreaming right now. Explain that she has dreams every night but does not notice she's dreaming, thus, how does she know if she is dreaming right now? This could spark her initial interest in lucid dreaming. If she is genuinely unsure whether or not she is dreaming, you could provide some clues to see if she can answer. Remind her that in dreams, it is possible to do things which are impossible in real life, such as push through a solid surface. Can she do that now? If not, then she must be awake. If she still seems confused and unable to determine whether or not she is dreaming, you could wait until she is a little older and try again, or cease trying to teach her. If she is able to determine that she is awake when you ask her, she has demonstrated that she is ready and able to participate in a lucid dreaming journey.

Asking your child to contemplate whether or not she is awake also serves to bring her attention to the present moment. Children tend to naturally be much more present-minded than adults, but they can still benefit from certain meditation practices such as taking deep breaths. In particular, asking children to take note of how their bodies feel can be very useful. Young children are still figuring out the sensations of hunger, thirst, fatigue, or the need to go to the bathroom. In times of difficult emotions, it can be fruitful to bring your child's awareness to bodily sensations, such that they are better able to identify what it is they are feeling both emotionally and physiologically. Older children and teens can benefit immensely from being trained in basic mindfulness techniques which will benefit them throughout their lives.

Teaching your child to lucid dream will naturally prepare her for learning mindfulness techniques as well. In particular, if you can teach your teen to pause during the most emotionally difficult moments of the day in order to perform reality checks and take deep breaths, she will certainly experience general benefits beyond an increase in lucid dream frequency. She will be building her emotional resilience and healthy coping skills as well.

Not much effort on your part is needed to teach your child to have lucid dreams. People under the age of eighteen sleep much more than adults do, and even spend more time in the REM stage of sleep than adults do. Simply put, your children are having more dreams than you are. It should come as no surprise, then, that children have more nightmares than adults do. Lucid dreaming could perhaps benefit children even more than it does adults, since children are still learning all about how to cope with all kinds of difficult situations and emotions.

13. Teaching Children to Lucid Dream

Young children are capable of experiencing awe over small aspects of life which adults gloss over and do not even notice. Imagine the awe that your child will experience in a lucid dream! Give her the gift of this awe-inspiring experience, as well as increased confidence which can be practiced in the realm of lucid dreams. Controlling dreams is mostly about controlling your own emotions, reactions, thoughts, and imagination. Think how these skills can benefit your child in waking life. The promise of having lucid dreams will likely be enough to convince your child to join you and participate in learning this skill.

Young children tend to have immense confidence, which unfortunately wears down over the years as they are faced with their own limitations and experience failures. Children, then, are less likely to face as many roadblocks as adults do when it comes to controlling their dreams. If you teach your child, in simple terms, that dreams are a figment of her imagination and therefore every aspect of those dreams can be controlled, she will believe you 100 percent. Doubt is less likely to plague her abilities as it likely affects yours. Do not even tell her about doubt; do not tell your children what to expect in a lucid dream. Give them the tools they need to explore this mind state, and let *them* teach *you*! They are likely to come around to the same conclusions you do without you needing to tell them anything more than how to achieve a lucid dream.

It is likely that just mentioning the concept of lucid dreaming will be enough for your child to have a lucid dream. Lucid dreamers should not be surprised when their children learn a skill such as lucid dreaming or even meditation at a faster pace than they do. Your children do not have the years of accumulated emotional baggage that you have. They are confident and eager to show you what they can do. It should not surprise us that lucid dreaming is a skill well suited for children to learn. There are other abilities, such as language acquisition and the ability to learn perfect pitch, which children far exceed adults in learning. Their brains are constantly growing and developing. Long stretches of REM sleep play an integral, vital role in that development.

The importance of REM sleep for learning has been demonstrated in countless scientific ways. To provide just one example, consider the fact that adults learning a new language experience an increase in the amount of time they spend in REM.[1] Babies, who are learning language at a remarkable rate, sleep for 12–16 hours a day and spend half their sleep in REM. Adults sleep 7 to 9 hours a night, spending only 20 percent of the night in REM. Our remarkable adult brains will respond to our intention to learn a language through an automatic increase in REM.

While all sleep phases are essential and each play vital roles in our health and well-being, only children have the joy of experiencing long stretches of REM sleep. Consider, then, just how important it is that you validate any difficulties your child has with nightmares, and provide effective techniques for dealing with nightmares.

Childhood is the best time in life to build a solid foundation of lucid dreaming skills, which can be carried into adulthood. Rather than shying away from teaching this skill to children, we should treat lucid dreaming like language acquisition or musical ear training. While these skills can be learned in adulthood, considerably more effort is needed to acquire them, and learning will occur at a slower pace.

Recall that lucid dreaming helps you learn to face your fears, value the time you spend sleeping, open new avenues for creative problem solving, and learn to practice awareness throughout your waking and dreaming life. What wonderful skills to teach your children! There is no time like the present to cultivate presence of mind.

Sleep Science and Philosophy

Lucid dreaming as a concept has far-reaching consequences for our understanding of the human brain, as well as our philosophical and spiritual belief systems. In this section, we will explore some of the most pivotal scientific research into sleep and dreams, as well as the kinds of philosophical and spiritual conclusions that some people have drawn from the concept of dreaming in general and lucid dreaming in particular.

14

What We Know: Scientific Data

*T*he primary goal of this book is to teach you how to lucid dream and how to improve the quality and frequency of your lucid dreams. I aim to sufficiently motivate readers to sustain their lucid dreaming practice, which you can think of as instituting a lifestyle change rather than a crash diet. That said, a secondary goal is to connect you with scientific research, both recent and historic, which will inform and improve your lucid dreaming practice.

The scientific study of sleep began rudimentarily in the late 19th century, and benefited significantly from electronic advances in technology that arose soon after. In 1928, psychiatrist Hans Berger was able to conduct the first electroencephalogram (EEG) recordings of sleeping individuals. Demonstrating the neurological state of sleep was essential for Berger in his attempt to prove that the signals recorded by the EEG originated in the brain and not from other sources such as muscles or movement. He was able to prove this by demonstrating how the EEG signals changed significantly once individuals fell asleep. This is part of how we know that sleep is a neurophysiological state distinct from wakefulness and involving significant brain activity. Prior to the onset of formal sleep science, such as Berger's research, many scientists posited that sleep was a period of little to no brain activity.

Huge strides were made in the 1950s when Eugene Aserinsky and Nathaniel Kleitman discovered, through EEG recording, periods of sleep with low-voltage, fast-wave brain patterns just as intense as those recorded in waking individuals. Aserinsky had, outside of the lab, noticed rapid eye movements in sleeping children. Aserinsky and Kleitman were able to prove that such rapid eye movements corresponded to a specific phase of sleep, thus leading to the discovery and naming of "REM sleep."

Other exciting progress was made, still in the 1950s, when Walter R. Hess demonstrated that it is possible to externally induce sleep through electrically stimulating the thalamus. This data proved that sleep results from a change in brain activity and not, as previously posited, through a cessation of brain activity. Later studies showed that activity in the brainstem is integral to the production of sleep. Overall, these initial brain studies shocked people by demonstrating that sleep is in fact a highly active time for the brain.

At this stage of sleep research, scientists began to discover a good deal about the four distinct sleep stages. For a number of reasons, understanding these stages can help you to better understand how dreams work. In particular, if you are interested in attempting a wake-induced lucid dream, it can be helpful to know when you are going to be in REM. I recommended in the chapter "Induction Techniques" that you begin attempting WILDs by setting an alarm for six hours into sleep.

Looking at the chart below, you will see why I recommended this. Notice that we cycle from non–REM to REM and back throughout the night, and that REM phases lengthen across the night, with the longest REM periods in the last two or more hours before waking. Even if you are not trying to have WILDs, keep in mind the importance of these morning hours before waking as potential periods for lucid dreams. For example, if you wake up naturally before your alarm, whether due to sound or your bladder or for an unknown reason, seize this opportunity! Whenever you wake up naturally but are able to go back to sleep, remember your intention to become lucid in a dream.

In this book, I focus heavily on REM sleep, since that is the phase in which most complex dreaming occurs. But each sleep phase plays its own distinct, vital role for our mental and physical health. I have spoken previously about the role REM sleep appears to play in learning and memory, for example, the fact that individuals learning a new language will experience an increase in REM sleep. REM sleep is not the only phase of sleep important for memory, however.

The deep non–REM sleep of phase 3 unfortunately deteriorates as we age. As Matthew Walker writes in *Why We Sleep*, this deterioration

Sleep Phases

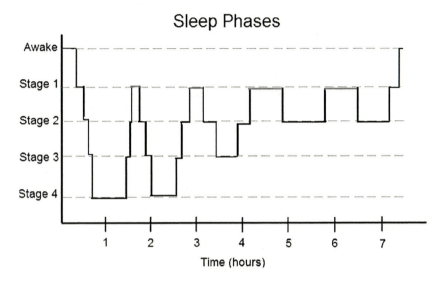

CC Creative Commons. Wikimedia Commons, *"Simplified Sleep Phases."*

"is linked to a decline in memory. However, if you assess a patient with Alzheimer's disease, the disruption of deep sleep is far more exaggerated. More telling, perhaps, is the fact that sleep disturbance precedes the onset of Alzheimer's disease by several years, suggesting that it may be an early-warning sign of the condition, or even a contributor to it."[1] Thus, my hope is that becoming a lucid dreamer will teach you to value not only REM, but sleep more generally, for the role it plays in your health. If you ever find your sleep quality significantly decreasing, see a doctor immediately and seek out ways to naturally improve your sleep without sleeping pills, which do not induce the same quality of sleep as natural methods do.

Every living species which has been studied has been proven to sleep, and Non-REM sleep is 500 million years old. Only mammals and birds have REM sleep, however, making REM sleep a more recent evolutionary innovation.[2] Smaller animals tend to have more REM, and more sleep in general, than larger animals. For example, elephants and giraffes sleep 3 to 5 hours a night whereas squirrels and bats sleep from 17 to 20 hours in a day. Altricial animals, such as humans, are born too immature to care for themselves. These animals experience high amounts of REM early in their lives, which decreases with age. Precocial animals, such as horses, can take care of themselves from birth. (To remember this term, think of the word "precocious," which means "mature for your age.") Foals can walk within hours of being born. Horses sleep a mere two and a half hours, on average, in a given twenty-four-hour period. They sleep in short bursts of about fifteen minutes, involving just five minutes of REM.

While every single animal that has been studied for signs of sleep has in fact been found to sleep, there is considerable variation in the composition of sleep across species. Consider the fact that sea mammals such as dolphins could not survive if they slept in the same way that humans do; they would stop swimming and sink to the deep ocean. How does their biology circumvent this? They experience unihemispheric sleep—sleeping with one half of the brain at a time. Birds also experience this type of deep, non–REM sleep, which takes place in one hemisphere at a time. Partially aquatic mammals, on the other hand, have a different approach. While on land, they experience both REM and non–REM sleep. In the ocean, they experience mainly non–REM sleep. It is still a point of scientific contention whether or not aquatic mammals such as dolphins and whales experience any REM sleep.

Sleep scientists also do not yet definitively agree on sleep and dreams' overall biological function for human beings, or other mammals for that matter, though they have made considerable strides in sleep research in the past several decades. J. Allan Hobson writes, "Among the likely active functions of sleep are the structural development of the brain in early life, the active maintenance of brain programs for instinctual behavior, and the active processing and storage in the brain of information acquired during waking experience."[3] In other words, sleep is essential for child development, memory, overall physiological health, and problem solving.

Dr. William Dement and Nathaniel Kleitman were the first to discover the precise role of eye movements during the REM phase of sleep. One of the participants in their 1957 study showed a persistent eye movement pattern, moving from left to right repeatedly. Upon waking, he reported that he had been dreaming about watching a table tennis game. This connection between eye movement and dream content provided the foundation necessary to scientifically prove the existence of lucid dreaming.[4]

Almost twenty years later, in 1975, Keith Hearn proved the existence of lucid dreaming in a laboratory. Experienced lucid dreamer Alan Worsley become lucid during sleep, and, under EEG observation, signaled a predetermined set of eye movements when he became lucid.[5] This data was soon verified by American researchers Stephen LaBerge and Lyn Nagel at the Stanford Sleep Laboratory through a similar study involving signaling via eye movements. These studies officially settled the debate over the existence of lucid dreaming, allowing for more interesting studies to be conducted in the coming years, investigating the phenomenon of lucid dreaming in more detail. The following chapters will cover some of what the scientific research of lucid dreaming has determined thus far, through experiential studies of individuals while they are lucid dreaming, as well as through survey data and analysis of dream reports.

15

Demographic Trends in Lucid Dreaming

*L*ucid dreams are rare. Most dreams are not lucid. Everyone has several dreams every night, whether they remember those dreams or not. For most people, none of those dreams are lucid. Even for the avid lucid dreamer, the vast majority of her dreams are not lucid.

Stephen LaBerge writes, "After a decade of experience with more than a thousand lucid dreams, I rarely have more than a few per month unless I have a conscious desire to have more."[1] If you make a strong, consistent, conscious effort, you might be able to have a lucid dream nearly every night. Even if that is the case, though, your nightly lucid dream will occur alongside many more non-lucid dreams.

As of the time of this writing, there are about a half dozen studies on the incidence of lucid dreaming in the general population. First, a 1988 study concluded that about 58 percent of the population has experienced a lucid dream at least once in their lifetime, and 21 percent of people have one or more lucid dream a month.[2] A 2011 study took data from 919 German adults and found that 51 percent had at least one lucid dream in their lifetime, and 20 percent had at least one a month.[3]

Several other studies were conducted between 1998 and 2011. These studies almost universally concluded that a majority of participants had at least one lucid dream in their lifetime, with a minority of participants reporting one or more lucid dreams per month. There is considerable variation in the numbers, though, with anywhere between 19 and 37 percent of participants reporting one or more lucid dreams per month.[4] In every case, the majority of participants did not report such frequent lucid dreams.

It appears from current research that most people have had at least one lucid dream in their lifetime, and yet lucid dreams are rare in the context of overall dream experiences. Much more research is needed to provide an answer to the following questions: How many people have had at least one lucid dream? How many people have one or more lucid dreams per month? The studies that exist seem to imply that the answers may differ along demographic lines, due to differences such as age and culture of participants, but more information is needed to investigate these demographic trends.

The only demographic trend that has proven significant and consistent across all studies conducted thus far is age. Multiple studies have concluded that younger individuals are more likely to report frequent lucid dreams, and they are more likely to report having had a lucid dream at some point in their lifetime, than older individuals are.

Age and Lucid Dreaming Frequency

I have already established that younger people are more likely to experience lucid dreams. But why? In "Lucid Dreaming by the Numbers," Kelly Bulkeley poses the following research question: "Are younger people more likely to experience lucid dreaming simply by virtue of being young, or is this particular generation of young people more likely to experience lucid dreaming?"[5]

I believe this phenomenon is more likely "by virtue of being young" than a factor for this generation of young people. Researchers have observed this trend as early as 1988. This trend has also been observed by researchers in different countries, so we are not just discussing one culture or geographic location when we state that younger people are more likely to report lucid dreams than older people are. My hypothesis that age itself is the major reason behind this trend has to do with differences in circadian rhythm, amount of sleep, and the ratio of REM to non–REM sleep across age groups. The following chart will help illustrate these factors.

You can see in the chart that the ratio of REM to non–REM changes across our lifetimes, with teens and adults experiencing less REM than children do. As we age, the biological features of circadian rhythm,

Sleep Patterns and Age

	Ratio of REM to Non–REM	Total Hours of Sleep	Schedule	Circadian Rhythm
Infants	50/50	12–16	Polyphasic	Sleep in periods of 1–4 hours throughout the day.
~3 years old	30/70	10–13	Biphasic	Early to bed with a day-time nap.
Late child-hood	30/70	9–12	Monophasic	Early to bed compared to adults—sleep onset before 9 p.m.
Teens	20/80	8–10	Monophasic	Late to bed compared to adults—sleep onset by 12 a.m. or later.
Adulthood	20/80	7–9	Monophasic	Sleep onset between 9 p.m. to 12 a.m.

including the production of melatonin, also decrease, leading to less sleep over time as well. This is an unfortunate fact of life that occurs for a variety of reasons.

Researchers and doctors use the term "sleep efficiency" to refer to the ratio of time you slept versus the time spent in bed. If you slept 8 of the 8 hours you were in bed, you had 100 percent efficiency. Late middle-aged and elderly individuals are rarely so lucky, as sleep efficiency decreases with age. There is a common misconception that older adults need less sleep than younger adults. This is unequivocally untrue. Older adults are less *able* to sleep; that does not mean they need less sleep. In *Why We Sleep*, Matthew Walker points out that 100 years ago, less than 2 percent of the U.S. population slept for six or fewer hours per night. Now, nearly 30 percent of American adults are sleep deprived.[6] It's clear that the amount of sleep we *get* is far from the amount of sleep we *need*.

Overall, we simply dream less and less as we get older. We experience less REM sleep as teens and adults than we do as children, and the older we get, the worse our sleep efficiency becomes. This strikes me as at least part of the puzzle of why younger people report more lucid dreams than older people do.

One flaw in my hypothesis is that the surveys I referenced in the previous section all concerned adult participants exclusively. No one under the age of eighteen was surveyed. The youngest among these participants, however, were older teens and young adults getting much more sleep than the adults surveyed. Thus, those participants were sleeping and dreaming more than their older counterparts and were more likely to have lucid dreams as a result. These younger participants were also more likely to *remember* incidences of lucid dreams they had in childhood, from back when they were sleeping with extremely high efficiency, getting as much as eleven to twelve hours of sleep a night, and spending 30 percent of their night's sleep in REM.

This could, in part, explain why these younger participants were more likely than older participants to report having a lucid dream sometime in their life, in spite of the fact that they had thus far experienced shorter lifetimes overall than the older participants had. Perhaps these older participants had simply forgotten the lucid dreams of their childhood by the time they were asked the survey questions. My hope is that future research will investigate the question posed by Kelly Bulkeley. I recommend that more research be conducted on lucid dreaming incidence among people under the age of eighteen. The age trend may be even steeper than we currently realize.

16

Dreams and Video Games

*T*here are self-evident connections between dreams and video games and, in particular, between lucid dreams and video games. Both the dream state and video games could be described as virtual realities. The dreamer and the gamer are immersed and playing an active, participatory role in a reality that differs from the reality in which their body physically resides.

On a personal level, I have experienced and heard others discuss the impact that significant video game playing has on their dreams. I have had dreams based on the visual environment of games I've played, especially when I played these games frequently. In one such instance, I dreamt that I was playing the PlayStation game *Crash Team Racing*. I was watching and controlling my character's actions. However, unlike in the waking state, the entire field of my perception was the game environment. I could not feel or see my own body in front of a screen playing the game. There was no screen. Perspective is an interesting feature of dreams influenced by gaming, and it is one of many factors that have been researched.

A comparison between video games and lucid dreaming also brings to mind the aspect of control, a feature of many but not all lucid dreams. Similarly to the lucid dream state, in a video game, you are attempting to exert effective control over your surroundings, usually in order to defeat enemies, achieve feats, and acquire goods.

People sometimes remark that their dreams feel like video games, but from a historical perspective, it ought to be discussed the other way around. We could ask ourselves how much influence the dream state has had on the invention of video games, especially considering the role we know dreams have played in several inventions, works of art, and scientific discoveries.

16. Dreams and Video Games

In "A Deeper Inquiry into the Association between Lucid Dreams and Video Game Play," Gackenbach and Hunt draw upon new and preexisting research to discuss this connection from multiple angles. The researchers studied "hardcore" gamers, whom they defined as those who play several times a week for sessions of more than two hours, have played more than fifty games in their lifetime, and have played since at least the third grade. The researchers found that these gamers had more lucid dreams than those who infrequently or never game. Hardcore gamers also had a higher frequency of third-person perspective in their dreams.[1]

Overall, those with a history of frequent gaming are more likely to have lucid dreams, third-person perspective dreams, and effective dream control, than those who rarely game. The hardcore gamers also reported more metacognitive activity—reflecting on their own thoughts during the dream. Video games and lucid dreaming have both been positively correlated with improved spatial reasoning skills.

Gackenbach and Hunt also drew upon preexisting research and compared data of frequent gamers to data of frequent meditators. Frequent meditators, like frequent gamers, report more lucid dreams than control groups. In contrast, though, the day-to-day impact of these activities on dreams differs among gamers versus meditators. After a day of significant gaming, gamers have a higher level of dream control the following night. The researchers use the phrase "thwarted intent" to discuss this phenomenon. After gaming, gamers experience less "thwarted intent" in their dreams than they would after a day of not gaming. The meditators, however, experience *more* thwarted intent in their dreams after a day of significant meditating. So while both groups are more likely than their control groups to have lucid dreams, the activities of playing video games and meditating have a different impact on dream control. Once again, this proves to be another example of why it is important to separate the concepts of lucidity and control.

Another feature of dreams that researchers have studied is bizarreness. I often joke that when someone says she had a "really weird dream," that is a redundant phrase because all dreams are weird, especially if you really pay attention to them lucidly. But, of course, weirdness exists on a spectrum. Hardcore gamers tended to have a higher level of bizarreness in their dreams than infrequent gamers do.

In light of this research, I want to recommend a few actions for frequent and occasional gamers. I recommend tracking days of heavy video game play in your dream journal, in order to determine if the connection demonstrated through this research also applies to you. It will most likely take several weeks or months of data in order to determine whether heavy gaming is increasing your likelihood of lucid dreaming. If you wish, you can also track your own level of thwarted intent or dream control in dreams following a day of heavy gaming, to see if you are better able to control your dreams after a gaming day.

I do not recommend any kind of screen time immediately before bed, since the blue light from screens negatively impacts melatonin production and makes it harder to fall asleep. Further, I do not necessarily recommend trying to play video games as a means of having more lucid dreams. If you have no interest in video games, playing them does not seem like the ideal method of increasing lucidity, considering that there are so many other viable techniques at your disposal. That said, now that you are aware of a possible connection between these two hobbies, you can investigate that connection in your own life.

17

Out-of-Body Experiences and Astral Projection

*I*f you explore the topic of lucid dreaming in books and online, you are bound to run into information about the related topics of out-of-body experiences (OBEs) and astral projection (AP). While these experiences are not the focus of my book, I feel obliged to briefly cover them, so that readers have the background knowledge necessary to interact with information on these topics in a critical and informed manner.

OBEs and AP are topics rife with controversy and disagreement among the lucid dreaming community, including controversy around the very definitions of these words. Some people argue that both OBEs and AP are types of lucid dreams, while others argue that these are necessarily three distinct mind states. Some wish to avoid discussions of OBEs and AP in an attempt to preserve their reputation as skeptical, scientifically minded lucid dreamers, while others argue that OBEs and AP are phenomena that science can tackle.

In the interest of providing an unbiased introduction to the topic, I look to the dictionary for broad definitions of these terms rather than to any particular lucid dreamer's philosophical opinion. Merriam-Webster defines an out-of-body experience as "an experience in which a person has a feeling of being separated from his or her body and able to look at himself or herself and other people from the outside."[1]

Merriam-Webster defines astral projection as "the ability of a person's spirit to travel to distant places."[2] I, however, prefer the Lexico definition: "A paranormal phenomenon in which an individual's consciousness is said to leave the physical body temporarily or to move at will into some ethereal realm; an instance of this."[3]

It is interesting to me that Lexico uses the term "paranormal" to describe AP, but not in its description of an OBE. Some individuals claim that they are able to ascertain information from the actual, real, physical world through AP. Therefore, they categorize these experiences as "real" or, in other words, as not strictly occurring within their own minds. For interested readers, there are entire books on these topics. My focus has always been on lucid dreaming rather than the related topics of OBEs and AP.

I agree with the Lexico writers that AP ought to be considered a paranormal phenomenon, whereas lucid dreaming and OBEs should not. The phenomenon of lucid dreaming is completely consistent with all scientific laws. As I have argued previously, in many ways, a lucid dream is merely a thought. In order to not believe in lucid dreaming, you have to not believe it is possible for someone to have a particular thought—*I'm dreaming*—in a dream. Indeed, I find this disbelief to be more outlandish than the claim of lucid dreaming itself. Of course, all kinds of thoughts are possible in dreams, just as they are possible in waking life. Anyone who has taken note of the content of her own dreams can see that they contain streams of thought just as waking consciousness does.

Astral projection exists much more outside the realm of typical cognitive experience than lucid dreaming does. I believe that OBEs and AP are "real" in the sense that they are experiences people have. It is my opinion that these experiences occur within the psychological realm of the mind and the physiological realm of the brain and body, rather than the physical, external world.

Although I have never had an AP experience, I have, however, had one OBE. This would not have happened to me had I not been an avid lucid dreamer and explorer of the hypnagogic mind state. I used to be completely disinterested in OBEs and wanted to distance myself from the topic because I thought it tainted discussions of lucid dreaming. Then, in 2011, without making any attempt to do so, I happened to have an OBE following one of my lucid dreams.

Personally, I characterize OBE as a subphenomenon of lucid dreaming. I entered the OBE from sleep paralysis, in a matter that is highly similar to a wake-induced lucid dream. In spite of the fact that I did not seek out an OBE, and in spite of the fact that I don't believe I have a literal soul or entity that left my physical body during my OBE, my OBE is among the top five most profound and memorable lucid dreaming experiences I have ever had. I would be remiss to ignore this topic in my book, since, whether you are seeking the OBE experience or not, it could happen to you as you hone your lucid dreaming practice. It is preferable to go into such an experience with some background information, ideally more background information than I had at the time.

My OBE occurred on a Sunday morning. I was able to sleep in late that morning, and I had multiple awakenings. During these awakening periods, I practiced autosuggestion in an attempt to have a lucid dream. Here is my dream report from that morning:

Lucid, I find myself in a large gymnasium-like open room where one entire wall is a window, with columns. The window overlooks a city landscape with beautiful architecture, not based on any city in real life. The colors of the buildings are a light/muted brown, orange, white, and yellow. I'm amazed at my own imagination. I look out and see a man looking at me. I'm surprised. I expect him to jump off the roof he is standing on, and then he does. I'm not scared. I watch him land on another building below him. I keep looking out the window and move to the center of the room for the best view. I can no longer see very well. It feels like my eyes are watering. I'm afraid the dream is about to fade. I decide it would be a shame not to fly over the landscape. I realize I'll never see it again. I fly out the window and then all visual imagery fades to nothing. I am floating in black space. I feel as if I am floating up. I "realize" what's about to happen before it does. I think that I am going to float up into my real body and then wake up immediately.

I do float up toward my real body, but I do not enter it. I sense that my body is "near" me but I'm stuck and I feel nothing. Technically, at this point, I know I am in sleep paralysis, but I can't feel the paralysis because I can't feel my real body.

I hear a man's voice. It says, "Hi." I'm instantly terrified. I don't want other people around me while I am in this vulnerable state. There's nothing I can do about it. Then he says, in a mocking tone, "My name is Elliot." Immediately following this statement, I hear thousands of voices, many of which are my own voice, talking at once such that I cannot make out any individual words. Then visual hallucinations appear. I wake up by opening my eyes. I still see visual hallucinations of moving geometric patterns on my ceiling, which are intense for a few minutes before fading. At this point I have the distinct feeling that I am floating near the ceiling, several feet above my real body. I slowly float back down and, entering my real body again, wake up.

This dream demonstrates many principles discussed earlier in this book, such as the role of expectation in dreams, and the fact that attempting physical feats like flying as opposed to more passive, observant activities can cause the dream to fade or to speed up the process of fading.

While many OBE reports involve the individual entering an OBE while falling asleep, perhaps during an attempt at lucid dreaming, my OBE occurred as I woke from a lucid dream. The transitional processes of falling asleep and waking up cause similar phenomena. Take sleep paralysis, for example. It occurs either as you are falling asleep or as you are waking up.

Like sleep paralysis, and perhaps often with sleep paralysis, OBEs occur in the hypnagogic state, a liminal phase between wakefulness and dreaming. Executing WILDs, dreamers are asked to remain aware during the hypnagogic state as they fall asleep. It seems slightly less common for dreamers to notice the hypnagogic state as they are waking up, unless they are waking up from a lucid dream, experiencing sleep paralysis, or having an OBE. In my case, I transitioned from a lucid dream straight into an OBE, which I believe technically involved sleep paralysis, but I could not exactly feel the paralysis since I was not feeling body sensations and rather existed as a sort of point of awareness that I strongly felt to be *near* my physical body rather than inside it.

Perhaps even more so than lucid dreams and other psychic phenomena such as meditative states, OBEs test the limits of language. What do I mean when I say, "I was near my body"? What "I" do I speak of in that sentence? I choose to use the phrase "point of awareness" because it best conveys the experience, but this description is decidedly difficult to imagine for anyone who has not personally had an OBE. Even advanced lucid dreamers may struggle to comprehend my description, but it is the most accurate description I can give within the limits of the English language.

I would welcome further scientific research into AP and OBEs, specifically related to the latter, I would love for scientific researchers to investigate neurological activity during OBEs. Lucid dreaming is characterized by specific, detectable activity in the brain, namely gamma band activity between 25 and 40 Hz.[4] Are OBEs accompanied by the same gamma band activity? Or are they accompanied by their own specific, testable activity in the brain?

Furthermore, can AP and OBEs be differentiated by neurological activity, or would studying brain activity during these two mind states demonstrate that they are essentially the same? Such scientific research would be tricky as it would require participants who are able to astral project or have OBEs on command. But such research would help settle this debate over the definitions of the terms "lucid dream," "out of body experience," and "astral projection" in an objective way. In the following chapter I attempt to describe another topic that tests the limits of language as well as science: altered states of consciousness.

18

Lucid Dreaming as an Altered State of Consciousness

*I*n order to consider lucid dreams through the lens of altered states of consciousness, we first have to define an altered state of consciousness. People generally use the term to refer to experiences that humans have under the influence of psychoactive drugs, and we can most likely agree that drug experiences qualify as altered states. Others claim that they are able to reach an altered state of consciousness through meditation, prayer, trance, or other means.

The word "altered" indicates that these states are defined comparatively, through contrast with one's typical state of consciousness. For the vast majority of us, our normal, typical state of consciousness is one of sobriety and wakefulness. That said, dreaming consciousness is equally as natural as waking consciousness. The reason we tend to consider dreaming consciousness an altered state and waking consciousness the default state is because we spend the majority of our lives awake.

On average, people spend a third of their lives sleeping. Dreams primarily occur during REM sleep, which takes up approximately two hours out of an eight-hour rest. Thus, we spend a third of our lives sleeping, but only a quarter of that sleeping time in dreams. It is no surprise, then, that we consider the waking state, in which we spend two thirds of our lives, to be the normal state of consciousness, and the dreaming state in which we spend *one twelfth* of our lives, to be the unusual state.

Considering dreams as altered states, we can ask ourselves two important questions. To begin with, we can ask whether the mind states of lucid and non-lucid dreams are two distinct mind states, or if they are essentially the same kind of altered state. The second question one might ask is, what similarities might we find between the altered state of dreaming, whether lucid or not, and various altered states caused by psychoactive compounds?

Comparing Lucid and Non-Lucid Mind States

While it is self-evident that there are psychological and neurological differences between the waking and dreaming states, we are still left with the question of whether or not there are significant neurological differences between lucid and non-lucid dreams. Luckily, scientific researchers have put considerable effort into investigating this question.

Research by J. Allan Hobson and Edward F. Pace-Schott elaborates on the neuroscience of sleep well beyond what was previously known. They demonstrated that the REM phase of sleep is accompanied by a decrease in activity in the dorsolateral prefrontal and frontopolar cortices, while at the same time more blood flow is directed to the brainstem, limbic forebrain, and parietal operculum. What these neurological features of REM essentially demonstrate is a very different mind state than normal waking consciousness. This most likely comes as no surprise.[1]

Increased blood flow to the brainstem, forebrain, and parietal operculum partly explains the hallucinatory experience of dreams in REM. Decreased activity in the prefrontal and frontopolar cortices further explains the associated decrease in "metacognitive monitoring," which occurs during our dreams. This decrease in metacognitive activity involves "restricted volitional capabilities, impaired critical thinking, and a complete lack of insight into the true state of mind."[2]

This, too, most likely aligns with your personal experience of dreams as well as what you have learned in this book thus far. Lucid dreams are rare. Most of the time we do not have the critical thinking ability necessary to realize we are dreaming. In dreams, we have trouble executing even basic tasks like talking and walking. Thus we experience "restricted volitional capabilities," in other words, low levels of control, in non-lucid dreams. The "complete lack of insight into the true state of mind," which Filevich et al. discuss in their research, aligns with personal experiences we all have had in non-lucid dreams. The fact that in most dreams we assume we are awake, we believe impossible things to be true, and we generally do not even stop to notice these impossible things—this experiential lack of metacognitive functioning in dreams aligns with the neuroscientific explanation behind dreaming itself.

All of the above information, though, concerns non-lucid REM sleep. Are there neurological differences between non-lucid dreams and lucid ones? I have argued throughout this book that, while one must only realize she is dreaming in order to have a lucid dream, lucidity exists on a spectrum. Thus, in some dreams, you may technically be lucid but at a low level of lucidity. Understanding this spectrum of lucidity, and wishing to investigate the differences between non-lucid REM sleep and lucid dreams, researchers Ursula Voss and Georg Voss created the Lucidity and Consciousness in Dreams Scale.[3]

This self-report scale measures the factors of insight, realism, control, memory, thoughts, positive emotion, negative emotion, and dissociation in lucid and non-lucid dreams. These researchers concluded that non-lucid dreams have low values on all factors except realism. This supports my claim that real-seeming, vivid visual phenomena are not exclusive to lucid dreams and are in fact common in non-lucid dreams.

The researchers also investigated physiological and neurological features of lucid versus non-lucid dreams. They found that sleep atonia (muscle paralysis) and rapid eye movement bursts remained in lucid dreams, but that lucid dreams involved significant increases in gamma band activity. Gamma frequency is associated with "conscious awareness and executive ego functions."[4] These researchers therefore describe lucid dreams as a hybrid state of consciousness because it incorporates elements of regular, non-lucid REM sleep (such as muscle paralysis and rapid eye movement) as well as brain activity more commonly found in the waking state.

These researchers have gone on to harness the association between gamma band activity in an attempt to induce lucid dreaming by externally stimulating gamma band activity in order to mimic the neurology typical of a lucid dream. You will find more information on this in the final chapter of this book, "What We Don't Know: Questions for Further Inquiry."

Thus, while dreaming can be considered an altered state of consciousness in comparison to waking life, lucid dreaming specifically should be considered a separate and distinct altered state of consciousness. Lucid dreams have features in common with waking as well as with dreaming and thus remain in a category all their own. Anyone with an interest in altered states of consciousness should consider lucid dreaming in their investigation of the topic. Individuals who pursue altered states through drug use, trance, prayer, meditation or other means would be wise to utilize lucid dreaming—a safe, legal, healthy, and in fact beneficial altered state of consciousness.

Connection with Psychedelics

In the chapter "Dealing with Nightmares and Anxiety," I discussed the inherent similarities between nightmares and difficult hallucinatory experiences, arguing that they ought to be dealt with in a similar manner. In order to further explore the connection between psychedelic drugs and dreams, we must narrow down to specific psychoactive compounds that have commonalities with the dreaming states.

Psychedelic drugs such as lysergic acid diethylamide (LSD), psilocybin (magic mushrooms), dimethyltryptamine (DMT), and ayahuasca have much in common with the dream state, though considerably more research is needed to fully investigate these connections.

David Jay Brown wrote *Dreaming Wide Awake: Lucid Dreaming, Shamanic Healing, and Psychedelics,* which drew comparisons between lucid dreaming and psychedelics. From his research and observations, some compelling arguments for the connection between these topics include the idea that both psychedelics and lucid dreaming often involve synchronicity, synesthesia, and an immersion into an alternative reality. Both mind states are heavily impacted by our moods and thoughts during the experience. In the same way that a negative thought can turn your happy lucid dream into a nightmare, a dip in mood can turn a pleasant hallucinogenic trip into a difficult one. Finally, both states have spiritual implications for many people.[5]

Other connections between psychedelics and dream states are of a more philosophical nature. In the Tibetan tradition, dream yoga ultimately leads to sleep yoga, in which the goal is not simply to have lucid dreams but to achieve "clear light sleep." In clear light sleep, thought dissolves, and one does not experience a dream ego. Rinpoche describes it as follows: "When thought is observed in awareness with neither grasping nor aversion, it dissolves. When the thought—the object of awareness, dissolves, the observer or subject also dissolves."[6] One could compare clear light sleep state to the state known as ego death, which psychedelic users as well as meditation practitioners sometimes experience.

Ego death is exactly what it sounds like. It is the temporary dissolution of your own sense of self. When you experience an ego death, you lose all awareness of yourself as a self. You continue to be consciously aware, but you are no longer aware of your own ego, your own personality, your own clinging and rejecting of experiences. What often replaces your typical consciousness is a pleasant sense of connection. Rather than experiencing reality as a unique and separate self, you are aware of the interconnectedness of all life.

In "The Psychedelic Experience," a manual by Timothy Leary, Ralph Metzner, and Richard Alpert, the authors dive into various aspects of the psychedelic experience, including this dissolution of the self. The manual is based heavily on *The Tibetan Book of the Dead*, and in it, the authors expound on various connections that psychedelic drug experiences have in common with spiritual pursuits and meditation. They write,

> A psychedelic experience is a journey to new realms of consciousness. The scope and content of the experience is limitless, but its characteristic features are the transcendence of verbal concepts, of space—time dimensions, and of the ego or identity. Such experiences of enlarged consciousness can occur in a variety of ways: sensory deprivation, yoga exercises, disciplined meditation, religious or aesthetic ecstasies, or spontaneously. Most recently they have become available to anyone through the ingestion of psychedelic drugs such as LSD, psilocybin, mescaline, DMT, etc.[7]

While dreams are conspicuously absent from this list, I am confident that these authors would agree with the connection. Are psychedelics, meditation, and dream practices all pointing in the same direction: to the dissolution of boundaries, including the boundary of one's own sense of self? Leary, Metzner, Alpert, and many others seem to believe so. I tend to agree with them.

<h1 style="text-align:center">19</h1>

<h1 style="text-align:center">Additional Perspectives</h1>

*L*ucid dreaming is a multidisciplinary and potentially interdisciplinary area of study. You have learned thus far in this book that lucid dreaming can be studied on a neuroscientific level. You have seen the myriad ways in which it can be harnessed for psychological self-help. What's more, lucid dreaming has implications for both spirituality and philosophy. There are countless ways of looking at the topic of lucid dreaming. In this chapter we will explore some of those additional perspectives.

Philosophy

You have most likely come across a version of the following story, at some point in your life:

> Once upon a time, I, Chuang Chou, dreamt I was a butterfly, fluttering hither and thither, to all intents and purposes a butterfly. I was conscious only of my happiness as a butterfly, unaware that I was Chou. Soon I awaked [*sic*], and there I was, veritably myself again. Now I do not know whether I was then a man dreaming I was a butterfly, or whether I am now a butterfly, dreaming I am a man. Between a man and a butterfly there is necessarily a distinction. The transition is called the transformation of material things.

Chuang Chou, or Master Chang, lived around 369 to 286 BCE. Human beings have been baffled by the philosophical implications of dreams for thousands of years. As you have learned, most dreams are not lucid. Most of the time that a person has a dream, she believes the hallucination completely and may feel shocked to find that it was a dream.

Chuang Chou asserts that there is necessarily a distinction between a man and a butterfly. There is a difference, in fact many differences, between the waking state and the dream state. I do not think we should take from Chou's quote the idea that we are currently dreaming in the *exact same way* that we dream while asleep. Chou's comments more likely point to the fact that the dream state and the waking state should be considered equally real and valid experiences.

In his book *The Lucid Dreamer*, Malcolm Godwin astutely points out, "Too many mystics and enlightened beings have independently arrived at an understanding that our world is a dream for us to ignore what they say."[1] I do not intend to ignore what these mystics have said, but rather I mean to investigate both what they have said and what they may have meant precisely. I intend to do this by first investigating what the word "dream" may have meant to them in this particular context. If by the phrase "life is a dream," one means to say that life is illusory and impermanent, I certainly agree. If what one means to say is that dreams are no less real than waking life because all perception exists in our minds, I agree. If, however, these mystics are arguing that there are no differences whatsoever between the physiological states of waking and sleeping, I invite one of these people to fly before my eyes the way they would be able to in a dream.

More often than not, what people take away from various shortened versions of the butterfly story is the idea that we may now be dreaming and unaware of it. That is not what I take from this quote. To me, Chang's quote indicates that it does not make sense to assume waking reality is the truth, and dreams fiction, when it could just as easily be the other way around.

To argue that we may now also be dreaming in the same exact way that we dream in sleep, and that we may "wake up" from this dream too, actually hypothesizes a third mental state. We already know of two mental states: waking and dreaming. But if the waking state is really a kind of dream, there could be a third mental state of which we are currently unaware and that we could, in a sense, wake up to.

Note that the experience of waking up to this third mental state would not be exactly like waking from a dream in your current reality. Waking from a dream in your current reality is more like an act of remembering. You suddenly remember your "real" life, and remember that there are these two mental states and at any point you should consider which one you're experiencing. The mental states of waking and dreaming oscillate frequently—each and every day of our lives.

If I were to wake right now into a third mental state, it would either be a reality I have never previously known, or one I have somehow forgotten for the twenty-eight years of my life thus far. I would not think of dreams, waking reality, and possible other realities as *the same*. If there were no differences between the waking world and the dream world, why would we bother learning to lucid dream? What would it mean to discover that you're dreaming if there are no differences between dreaming and being awake? Even Chou asserts that there is "necessarily a distinction" between a man and a butterfly.

I believe there is value in looking at material reality as transient in the same way that dreams are transient, and recognizing the acts of falling asleep or waking up as a kind of "transformation of material things." There is value in considering the wakeful and dream states equally real, but the fact is that the two states are not *the same*. If you were to jump out of a window right now, you would not find yourself flying through the air.

I am not arguing that it is impossible that I'm currently dreaming, in the sense that there could be a third layer of consciousness of which I'm currently unaware. I am arguing that there is no possible way that I am dreaming in the way we normally use that word to mean. My body is not lying in bed unconscious and paralyzed while I write these words.

The argument I'm making in this chapter is a highly unpopular argument in lucid dreaming circles. Nevertheless, the further I go down the road of lucid dreaming, the more confident I am in my *wakefulness* whenever I am indeed awake. Beyond reality checks such as trying to float or to push through a solid surface, I have explored, over many years, features of the dream state that differentiate it from waking consciousness. These differences make it hard, indeed impossible, for me to conceptualize the wake and dream states as the same, even if long-standing spiritual traditions have rested upon such an argument.

Differentiating Dreams from Waking Consciousness

Some categories of difference between the waking and dreaming states include the way we ascertain information, the ways our emotions function, the appearance of our environment, and the influence we have over our environment. I am currently able to back up one of these categories with scientific evidence; the rest I have concluded based on extensive personal observation of the dream state while lucid.

Ascertaining Information

In waking life, we ascertain new data largely from our external environment. In other words, people tell us information, we read information, we hear information, we sense information visually. We ascertain data through our five senses, through our perception of external stimuli. This certainly also occurs in dreams, in spite of the fact that the stimuli, though it appears external, is in fact internally generated.

However, in dreams, we often ascertain new information purely from our thoughts. Have you ever had a dream in which you had a "sudden realization" of information? For example, you may suddenly realize you've been fired from your job, or you live somewhere new, or someone has died, or the planet you live on is under attack. No one told you the information and you did not read it anywhere. You may have ascertained the information visually, but even in this case, you have done so in an entirely different way than you would in waking life. In dreams, we often make wild assumptions based on very little actual data. For example, in a dream you may look around your strange house and "realize" that you have moved. This is not how we learn information in waking life. We would remember having moved houses. Or we would look for another explanation.

Instead, in the dream, when you "realize" something, this is a form of hallucination. In waking life, we do, of course, sometimes realize things mentally, but this process takes a different form. You may realize a mental conclusion based on a set of factual givens, for example, in solving a math problem. Or you may come to a personal realization, such as *I haven't been hanging out with my friends enough and my mood has lowered.* This is a purely mental realization, but it is subjective (unlike the dream realization *I've been fired from my job!*) and it is still based on external facts (I have not been hanging out with my friends, my mood has dipped).

After several years of lucid dreaming practice I began to notice this phenomenon of how learning works in dreams. Since noticing this, I have on countless occasions used this distinction between dreaming and waking to become lucid in a dream. This is a purely mental process of becoming lucid. The process goes like this: *My father is dead.* This thought comes out of nowhere, is based on nothing external, but feels entirely real. The emotion of grief is so strong and overpowering that I am nearly caught up in it, but I manage to stop and question the thought. *Wait, how do I know that? No one told me this. My father isn't here so how can I know if he's dead? This must be a dream. This is how I "realize" information in dreams.*

This process is so subtle that if you have not been practicing lucid dreaming for very long, you may not have yet noticed it. The information that appears suddenly in your mind may be emotionally distressing, which contributes to the difficulty you will have in noticing that you have no proof of the information.

Emotional Functioning

That brings me to the next category of difference between waking and dreaming, that is, the ways in which our emotions function in the two states. I have mentioned throughout this book the fact that our amygdala is 30 percent more active during REM sleep than it is during waking life. So, to begin with, our emotions tend to be stronger during dreams than waking life.

Beyond this scientific fact, I have anecdotally observed differences in the way my emotions function between the two states. Emotional functioning is likely to be a subjective and personal matter, though. I encourage you to be a true oneironaut, and take note of any differences you can find in your own emotional functioning in dreams versus waking life. This information may provide helpful clues for becoming lucid.

Personally, I find that in dreams, unlike in life, my emotions tend to precede events. Much the same way that information appears out of nowhere, emotions can arise from no external source. The usual cause and effect of event and emotion can be flipped in the dream. For example, I may feel suddenly frightened, and *then* a frightful image appears. I may feel distraught and aggrieved, and *then* "discover" (again, often usually without adequate evidence) that someone close to me has died or is sick.

Again, that is my own personal experience. Someone with a mood disorder, to name one example, may have a very different relationship with her own waking and dreaming emotions than I do. Just know that differences between waking and dreaming emotional function exist, and the sooner you take note of these differences, the sooner you can harness them as a means of becoming lucid.

Perceptual Differences

Perhaps the most obvious and noticeable category of difference between waking and dreaming states is the appearance of our environment—visual, auditory, tactile, olfactory, and gustatory perceptions. My findings in this area are again based on personal exploration, and I have primarily studied visual perception in the dream state, simply because it is for me the strongest and most noticeable type of perception in the dreaming realm.

The chief difference between waking visual perception and dreaming visual perception is that dream images are unstable. This is the case for fairly obvious reasons. Solid, non-digital, non-living objects do not typically move, shape-shift, change colors, or otherwise morph in waking life. If you are awake, and the walls of your house suddenly change color, you are hallucinating. You have either taken a drug or you are having an unusual mental event. In the dream state, however, these shifts are commonplace for anyone who pays enough attention to notice them.

Here is an example to which most people can relate. You have a dream about your brother, but he is also, somehow, your boss. You dream about your best friend, but she is also a character from a television show you've been watching. What exactly do people mean when they say they have dreamt this way, of two people merging into one? If you pay close, lucid attention to these dreams as they unfold, you will notice exactly how the merging occurs. If your brain is anything like mine, or if this phenomenon is universal, the morphing goes like this: You are talking to your best friend, then you look away at something else. When you look back, you are now speaking to the television character. Perhaps some of the physical features of each person are blended together, such that the television character has your friend's hair or clothing. The ways in which this person speaks to you may also be blended in some fashion, such that she is talking a bit like your friend and a bit like this television character.

What is happening here? On a neurological level, why are these occurrences so common? My hypothesis is that these doppelganger dreams occur because the visual elements of a dream are always shifting. People, places, and things are not stable as they are in waking life. They morph, they change, and if you aren't lucid or even if you are simply not paying close enough attention, you won't notice them changing. You will go from talking to your friend, to talking to a television character, and you won't notice the anomaly at all until you wake up.

I have dedicated hundreds of lucid dreams to studying exactly how dreams work, as an explorer of my own consciousness. In one lucid dream, I had made a plan to do nothing in the dream except watch. I stood in one spot and looked around the room in which I found myself. I stayed calm in order to prolong the lucid dream. I noticed that absolutely nothing was stable. Eventually, if I looked at one object for long enough, it changed in some subtle way.

My argument, which is based on personal experience and cannot be proven without considerable scientific substantiation, is that all dreams function this way, whether or not we realize it. In the lucid dreaming community, there is an understanding that you cannot read in dreams, because the external text will not stay put. Letters move or shift. If you look away, when you look back, the words have changed. Again, this is because nothing is visually stable in a dream. There is no "real" external environment. Everything is a product of your own mind, and as long as neurons continue to fire, emotions continue to emerge, expectations continue to change, and thoughts continue to occur, these mental events will affect the external environment. Dreams can only stay as still as your own mind.

The impossible nature of reading a book in your sleep ought not to be surprising, since the book isn't really there! Unless you have memorized an entire text and are capable of holding that text visually stable in your mind for many minutes, of course you cannot read a book in your dreams. If you close your eyes right now and try to read a book, can you? Perhaps an advanced meditator could have a visually stable dream if she made a conscious effort to do so. Take a moment to imagine what such a dream would entail. Once becoming lucid, the dreamer would have to survey the external environment and make sure to keep her thoughts and emotions stable enough so as not to interfere with the visual environment.

While I've noticed that some element of the visual field eventually will shift, it is hard to say with certainty how much time passes between each perceptual shift. (Research by Stephen LaBerge and his team showed that lucid dreamers, when asked to estimate a ten-second interval during sleep, were within a few seconds of their waking estimates.[2] On the other hand, though, conflicting research from Daniel Erlacher and his colleagues showed his research subjects taking twice as long to carry out activities in dreams than they did in reality.[3])

Eventually, I decided to investigate even further. In one of these observational lucid dreams, I walked over to a plain white wall. How much could a plain white wall possibly change? I looked closely at it, again with my intention to exist merely as an observer, not trying to change anything about the dream, letting the dream do what it wished and be what it was. I tried also to store as much information about this experience as I could, knowing that dreams are difficult to remember upon waking.

I observed the white wall for perhaps thirty seconds before patterns began to emerge. I could not have consciously created these patterns. Years later I still remember that the image was of primarily green and red dots, which formed geometric shapes that moved constantly. Within the dream, at this moment, I felt utterly convinced that this moving, changing, and shifting was the underlying rule of all dreams. I reiterate that I cannot prove this hypothesis. Instead I hand it over to you, the reader, to explore in your dreams. Perhaps this is specific only to my own dreams, or perhaps some readers will find it to be true for them as well.

I encourage all readers to view the dream state as a place you go to, to learn as much as you can about how it functions, and come back with new and interesting ideas, inventions, and perspectives. Your ideas do not have to align with mine. The joy is in the discovery. I am not the only person to argue something along these lines. In *The Tibetan Yogas of Dream and Sleep*, Rinpoche points out that most Westerners view dreams from a psychological standpoint. Plenty of us do not think very much about dreams at all, and if we do, we may do so through the lens of psychological self-improvement, analyzing the meanings behind our dreams. I am in agreement with Rinpoche, who writes, "Rarely is the nature of dreaming itself investigated. When it is, the investigation leads to the mysterious processes that underlie the whole of our existence, not only our dreaming life."[4]

While I again resist the tendency to describe waking and dreaming as the same, I do in fact agree with Rinpoche's hypothesis that the underlying process of dreaming reflects the underlying process of waking life. I agree with Rinpoche and other spiritual teachers and philosophers who argue for the importance of recognizing connections between waking and dreaming states. That said, I see value in not only comparing but also *contrasting* dreams and waking life.

Through personal investigation of my dreaming mind, I identified *change* as the underlying rule of dreams. One could say that I essentially stumbled upon what "English-speaking" Buddhists refer to as impermanence. Nothing in our waking life remains the same over time, either, though it may take longer to notice your waking life shifting as it tends to do so at a slower pace than dreams do.

While the desk I am looking at while writing this book is not changing color, shifting, or disappearing as it would in a lucid dream, it is an impermanent object, subject to change and deterioration over time. Thus, while my lucid dreaming practice is a practice of differentiating the dream state and the waking state, naturally I also make connections between the two. My theory on the importance of lucid dreaming to treat nightmares and anxiety rests upon a similarity between the dreaming mind and the waking mind, dreaming reality and waking reality. In both states, I argue, our anxieties are largely imagined. This fact is simply easier to comprehend in the dreaming state, but it is no less true in the waking state. Perhaps impermanence is the same way: it is always true, but it is particularly easy to witness in the dream state.

The nature of dreaming itself can lead you, as Rinpoche argues, to a greater understanding of existence more generally. The nature of sleeping is of scientific, biological, and psychological importance. We spend a third of our lives in this state, a state that, from a survival standpoint, is quite dangerous. We are paralyzed during much of sleep, and unaware of our surroundings. There must be a very good reason, or more likely, countless good reasons, for us to spend so much of our lives in this state.

The Mind's Impact

The final category of distinction I have found between waking life and dreams is the impact that your mind has on the environment. People often refer to this feature as "control" of the dream, but this phenomenon goes far beyond the realm of conscious control. In a lucid dream, yes, you may decide that you want to see a particular person or object and can make that person or object suddenly appear through conscious effort. Beyond conscious control there is also the general impact that your thoughts have on your external environment, which I have discussed throughout this book.

In dreams, your expectations create your reality in a very real, linear, and noticeable way. Ultimately, dream work may lead you to the conclusion that your mind has a similar influence over your waking life. We refer to the impact of our expectations over our waking life as "self-fulfilling prophecies." I believe that self-fulfilling prophecies are far-reaching, and that we each have a greater impact on our external reality than we tend to realize.

It is worthwhile to practice metacognitive activities such as meditation and lucid dreaming in order to learn more about your mind's impact on your external reality. That said, there are differences between the way your mind impacts reality in a dream versus the way it impacts reality in waking life. In dreams, you can literally make objects and people appear, disappear, and morph. Although your thoughts and emotions have a strong impact on waking reality, you do not have these powers in waking life, which would in fact be considered magic.

Advanced lucid dream work can lead to a feeling that waking life is more similar to dreams than previously thought, but the notion that we will awaken from our waking life into something else is, to me, a separate notion. I am not saying it is an untrue argument, merely a separate one. If nothing else, one day we will die, and perhaps this will function as a sort of awakening into a separate and previously unknown reality, one that is just as real as this one.

For now, in your waking life, I recommend that you view your dreaming practice as a means of becoming increasingly aware of the differences between waking and dreaming states. Lucid dreaming should make you more confident, not less confident, that you are awake when you are. This practice gives you the tools to differentiate between the two states of waking and dreaming, even as you discover surprising similarities between them, and even as you may also wonder whether there are more layers to consciousness than meets the eye. My recommendation can be summed up in the Latin saying "Dormiens vigila." *While sleeping, watch.*

The Spiritual Perspective

Many people share an interest in two or all three of the following pursuits: lucid dreaming, spirituality, and meditation. The Tibetan tradition of sleep and dream yoga connects all of these concepts. The practice of dream yoga is ancient. Scientific investigation of lucid dreaming only began in the 1970s. Significant, groundbreaking research into sleep states only began in the 1950s. If you have an interest in lucid dreaming, it is worthwhile for you to spend some time considering insight from cultures where people have studied lucid dreaming for much longer than Westerners have, even though the differences in culture and language can make these insights difficult to decipher and fully comprehend from an outsider's perspective.

It is difficult in our busy, modern culture to make time for just about anything, especially the less-understood spiritual pursuits. As Rinpoche points out, though, "There is always time for sleep; the third of our lives we spend sleeping can be used for practice."[5] You can use that time any way you wish: for pure enjoyment, for creativity and problem solving, for psychological healing, or as practice for waking life.

Sleep and dream yoga is a form of preparation for death. It overlaps with mindfulness practice because the aim of both practices is for the individual to cultivate a high level of awareness and focus on the present moment. In sleep and dream yoga, considerable attention is paid to the transitions between waking and dreaming, dreaming back to waking, and, ultimately, from either of these states into the transition of death.

Whatever death is, it is undeniably a transition. Whatever your ideas about death and afterlife currently are, you are free to try to conceptualize death through a lens of sleep yoga, which may help you prepare for this ultimate transition that we all have to make. Dream yoga, mindfulness, and lucid dreaming practices are all concerned with the concept of awareness. The practice of lucid dreaming, whether you are practicing it for spiritual or secular pursuits, is best achieved through increasing awareness during periods of transition. One of the ultimate goals of lucid dreaming practice, and also of mindfulness, is to maintain a continuity of awareness throughout your entire day and night.

There is reason to believe that death will function as a kind of transition similar to waking up or falling asleep. Without practicing lucid dreaming, dream yoga, or meditation in our waking lives, we are likely to execute the transition of death with the same lack of awareness with which we typically fall asleep or wake up.

Rinpoche argues that this preparation for death through increased awareness in life is ultimately the most important aspect of sleep and dream yoga. That said, he does not disagree with individuals using lucid dreaming in order to improve their waking lives in more temporary ways. These pursuits include improving one's own physical and mental health, which Rinpoche recognizes as worthwhile goals. However, he argues, "While the use of dream yoga to benefit us in the relative world is good, it is a provisional use of dream. Ultimately we want to use dream to liberate ourselves from all relative conditions, not simply to improve them."[6]

Whether you wish to improve conditions in your "relative world," or you wish to liberate yourself from these conditions completely, the method is the same: cultivate greater awareness throughout your life, and ultimately you can achieve continuity of awareness through all transitions between sleep, waking, and beyond.

20

What We Don't Know: Questions for Further Inquiry

Countless questions on sleep and dreams still remain unanswered by science. In this final chapter I will leave you to ponder some of the most pressing open questions in lucid dreaming research.

Do Lucid Dreamers Share Personality Traits?

One open research question that particularly interests me has to do with personality and lucid dreaming. The potential connection between personality and lucid dreaming could be explored a number of different ways. One could look at a sample of frequent lucid dreamers, who have lucid dreams every month, and compare them to a sample of people who rarely lucid dream. Alternatively, researchers could investigate whether there are shared personality traits among "natural lucid dreamers," those who are able to lucid dream without being taught the skill.

As previously mentioned in this book, there has in fact been research on differences in dream recall as it relates to personality. This study found that high dream recall is positively correlated with openness to experience and unrelated to the other Big Five personality traits (conscientiousness, extraversion, agreeableness, and neuroticism). While dream recall is not the same thing as lucid dreaming, and more research is needed into direct correlations to lucid dreaming, high recall is a precursor to lucid dreaming. Therefore, those with a high level of openness to experience are more likely to dream lucidly than those who score low on this trait.

Watson's study also demonstrated that "individuals who are prone to absorption, imagination, and fantasy" report more dreams than those who are less prone to such mental activities. This is not surprising, given what we know about the connections between video games, meditation, and lucid dreaming.[1]

One particular study conducted by Balgrove and Hartnell found that frequent and occasional lucid dreamers scored higher than non-lucid dreamers on Levenson's locus of control scale. Locus of control is a measurement of the degree to which people believe they have control over their lives. Someone with a high internal locus of control believes that her actions have a significant impact on her life, whereas someone with a high external locus of control believes that the circumstances of her life are largely determined by external factors.

Throughout this book I have explored the connection between lucid dreaming and dream control. While I tend to argue that it is unnecessary to exert control over a lucid dream, I find it unsurprising that lucid dreamers tend to believe that they have a high degree of control over the events in their lives. Becoming lucid in the first place is one way to exert control over the typically out-of-control world of dreams.

Frequent lucid dreamers in Balgrove and Hartnell's study also scored higher on tests of their "need for cognition," which is the degree to which individuals are inclined towards effortful cognitive activities. Given the fact that lucid dreaming is itself an effortful cognitive activity, these results are also unsurprising to me. Finally, frequent lucid dreamers also scored higher on Gough's self-assessed Creative Personality scale than non-lucid dreamers did. Thus, lucid dreamers consider themselves creative.[2]

From the aforementioned two studies, we can conclude that lucid dreamers tend to be imaginative, seek out effortful cognitive activities, consider themselves relatively in control over the events in their lives, and consider themselves to be creative. I assert that much more could be discovered about the personality traits of frequent lucid dreamers and natural lucid dreamers. In particular, I wonder whether lucid dreamers tend to report high, low, or average levels of anxiety.

Age and Lucid Dreaming

While we know that young people report more lucid dreams than older people do, scientists have not proven *why* this is. In general, lots of questions remain to be answered about the lucid dreaming abilities of children. From a legal and ethical standpoint, it is much easier to conduct scientific studies on adults. I am personally curious to know whether children would report even more frequent lucid dreams than their young adult counterparts, and whether or not children would report a high level of control over their lucid dreams. I further wonder if children would be able to learn the skill of lucid dreaming more quickly than adults, if provided with the same resources for learning the skill. I suspect that children are especially apt lucid dreamers, but as of yet there are no scientific studies to support my hypothesis.

Can Lucid Dreaming Be Induced through External Means?

The question of whether scientists could automatically induce lucidity in a dreaming research participant is among the most fascinating and pertinent questions in this field. For one thing, countless people are dying to be able to create, or to purchase, an external device that could reliably induce lucidity in users. While there are currently a handful of technological devices that claim to induce lucidity, none of these devices work 100 percent of the time, or even close to 100 percent of the time. While I believe that an external device will never replace the life-enriching practice of learning how to lucid dream, this is an undeniably pressing question for the sleep science community.

Researchers have determined that the hybrid mental state of lucid dreaming is accompanied by lower gamma frequency activity, specifically synchronous oscillations between 25 and 40 Hz. This neurological activity is associated with higher-level, metacognitive thinking, and is therefore not typically present during REM sleep. Understanding this correlative connection, researchers Ursula Voss et al. sought to determine whether lucid dreaming causes such gamma activity, or whether gamma activity leads to lucid dreaming.

The researchers stimulated low-frequency gamma band activity during REM sleep, and gathered dream reports from the participants to compare their neurological activity with subjective reports of lucidity. The researchers found that 58 percent of participants stimulated at 25 Hz reported lucid dreams, and 77 percent of participants stimulated at 40 Hz dreamed lucidly. Out of 324 total times that participants were stimulated, in 89 cases the subjects did not provide a dream report and in 28 cases they spontaneously awoke from REM. I find it interesting that 28 participants woke spontaneously, as premature awakening is a common roadblock in lucid dreaming. I have to wonder if these individuals did have a brief lucid dream, perhaps without remembering and reporting one. In any case, clearly there is potential to stimulate lucid dreaming externally. The researchers stated that this methodology could potentially help individuals with Post-Traumatic Stress Disorder to achieve lucidity during nightmares in order to alter their dream content.[3]

Seventy-seven percent is a fairly high rate of lucidity. Clearly there is potential for this technology to be harnessed and possibly sold to anyone interested in achieving lucid dreams. That said, it is my belief that no technology will succeed in achieving high-level, controlled, successful lucid dreams on command. While it's possible that a technological device could help dreamers to initially achieve lucidity, as you have learned by now, that is only the first step in lucid dreaming. Maintaining lucidity and successfully achieving what you set out to do in your lucid dreams are skills that no device can impart for you. Furthermore, the act of harnessing your own awareness through lucid dreaming and meditation will do much more to improve your mental health than simply achieving lucidity through an external device.

Your Role

It is my hope that all readers will continue to diligently write in their dream journals, check their mental states in times of stress, and use lucid dreaming as a means to mitigate fears and anxiety in their waking lives as well as their sleeping lives. I hope that lucid dreaming will enrich your life and that you, in turn, will contribute to the field of lucid dreaming through your personal exploration. There's no telling what the future of sleep science holds for the subfield of lucid dreaming. You can help move that scientific research forward by continuing to act as a citizen scientist, taking diligent notes, and exploring the vast realm of your own psyche. Even the simple act of experiencing frequent lucid dreams is a rare feat that moves this scientific field forward through an increased awareness and understanding of the strange phenomenon of lucid dreaming. Lucid dreams are among the best memories and experiences of my lives. I sincerely hope that readers can experience this realm of vast freedom, and experience greater calm in their waking lives as a result.

Chapter Notes

Chapter 1

1. Brigitte Holzinger, "Lucid Dreaming in Psychotherapy," in *Lucid Dreaming: New Perspectives on Consciousness in Sleep*, ed. Ryan Hurd and Kelly Bulkeley, Volume 1, Science, Psychology, and Education (Santa Barbara, CA: ABC-CLIO, 2014), 43.

2. B. A. Sharpless and J. P. Barber, "Lifetime Prevalence Rates of Sleep Paralysis: A Systematic Review," *Sleep Medicine Reviews* 15, no. 5 (2011): 311–315. doi:10.1016/j.smrv.2011.01.007.

3. T. A. Nielsen, D. L. McGregor, A. Zadra, D. Ilnicki, and L. Oullet, "Pain in Dreams," *Sleep* 16, no. 5 (August 1, 1993), http://doi.org/10.1093/sleep/16.5.490

Chapter 2

1. T. Wangyal and M. Dahlby, *The Tibetan Yogas of Dream and Sleep* (Delhi: Motilal Barnardsidass, 2004), 81.

Chapter 3

1. David Watson, "To Dream, Perchance to Remember: Individual Differences in Dream Recall," *Personality and Individual Differences* 34, no. 7 (2003): 1271–1286.

2. Karen Bolla, Suzanne R. Lesage, Charlene E. Gamaldo, David N. Neubauer, Frank R. Funderburk, Jean Lud Cadet, Paula M. David, Antonio Verdejo-Garcia, and Amy R. Benbrook, "Sleep Disturbance in Heavy Marijuana Users," *Sleep* 31, no. 6 (2008): 901–908, https://doi.org/10.1093/sleep/31.6.901

3. Jayne Gackenbach and Harry T. Hunt, "A Deeper Inquiry into the Association between Lucid Dreams and Video Game Play," in *Lucid Dreaming: New Perspectives on Consciousness in Sleep*, ed. Ryan Hurd and Kelly Bulkeley, Volume 1, Science, Psychology, and Education (Santa Barbara, CA: ABC-CLIO, 2014), 9.

4. Stephen LaBerge, *Exploring the World of Lucid Dreaming* (New York: Random House, 1990), 43–46.

Chapter 4

1. Elisa Filevich, Martin Dresler, Timothy R. Brick, and Simone Kühn, "Metacognitive Mechanisms Underlying Lucid Dreaming," *Journal of Neuroscience* 34, no. 3 (January 21, 2015): 1082–1088, doi:10.1523/JNEUROSCI.3342–14.2015.

2. Ursula Voss and Georg Voss, "A Neurobiological Model of Lucid Dreaming," in *Lucid Dreaming: New Perspectives on Consciousness in Sleep*, ed. Ryan Hurd and Kelly Bulkeley, Volume 1, Science, Psychology, and Education (Santa Barbara, CA: ABC-CLIO, 2014), 26–27.

3. LaBerge, *Exploring the World of Lucid Dreaming*, 64.

4. Ibid., 75.

5. P. McNamara, "The Dream Lag Effect: Dreams Participate in Memory Consolidation," *Psychology Today*, accessed May 20, 2019, https://www.psychologytoday.com/us/blog/dream-catcher/201105/the-dream-lag-effect.

Chapter 5

1. David Brown, *Dreaming Wide Awake: Lucid Dreaming, Shamanic Healing, and Psychedelics* (Randolph, VT: Park Street Press, 2016), 155–199.

173

2. Keith Hearne, "Lucid Dreams: An Electrophysiological and Psychological Study," unpublished PhD thesis, University of Hull (1978), 36.

Chapter 6

1. Jayne Gackenbach, R. Crandon, and C. Alexander, "Lucid Dreaming, Witnessing Dreaming, and the Transcendental Meditation Technique," *Lucidity Letter* 5 (1986): 34–40.

Chapter 7

1. Kelly Bulkeley, *An Introduction to the Psychology of Dreaming*, 2nd ed. (Santa Barbara, CA: Praeger, 2017), 68–70.

Chapter 8

1. Peter Bergmann, "8 Things the Mushroom Told Terence McKenna," accessed September 13, 2019, http://www.mckennite.com/articles/voice.

Chapter 9

1. Brown, *Dreaming Wide Awake*, 97.
2. E. J. Wamsley, M. Tucker, J. D. Payne, J. A. Benavides, and R. Stickgold, "Dreaming of a Learning Task Is Associated with Enhanced Sleep-Dependent Memory Consolidation," *Current Biology* 20, no. 9 (2010): 850–855, doi:10.1016/j.cub.2010.03.027.
3. Lee Irwin, "Memory, Meaning, and Imagination in Lucid Dreams," in *Lucid Dreaming: New Perspectives on Consciousness in Sleep*, Volume 1: Science, Psychology, and Education (Santa Barbara, CA: ABC-CLIO, 2014), 106–112.
4. Brown, *Dreaming Wide Awake*, 48–55.

Chapter 10

1. Matthew P. Walker, *Why We Sleep: Unlocking the Power of Sleep and Dreams* (New York: Scribner, 2017), 296.
2. Bulkeley, *Introduction to the Psychology of Dreaming*, 35.

3. Wangyal and Dahlby, *Tibetan Yogas of Dream and Sleep*, 62.
4. Calvin Hall and Robert Van de Castle, *The Content Analysis of Dreams* (New York: Appleton-Century-Crofts, 1966), 95–96.
5. Bulkeley, *Introduction to the Psychology of Dreaming*, 88.

Chapter 12

1. James F. Page, "Lucid Dreaming as Sleep Meditation," *New Perspectives on Consciousness During Sleep* Vol. 1: 67.
2. Gackenbach et al., "Lucid Dreaming," 34–40.
3. Jon Kabat-Zinn, "Defining Mindfulness." https://www.mindful.org/jon-kabat-zinn-defining-mindfulness/.

Chapter 13

1. J. De Koninck et al., "Intensive Language Learning and Increases in Rapid Eye Movement Sleep: Evidence of a Performance Factor," *International Journal of Psychophysiology* 8, no. 1 (1989), doi:10.1016/0167-8760(89)90018-4.

Chapter 14

1. Walker, *Why We Sleep*, 1567.
2. Walker, Why We Sleep, 56–60.
3. J. Allan Hobson, *Sleep* (New York: Scientific American Library, 1995), 21.
4. William Dement and Nathaniel Kleitman, "The Relation of Eye Movements during Sleep to Dream Activity: An Objective Method for the Study of Dreaming," *Journal of Experimental Psychology* 53, no. 5 (1957), doi:10.1037/h0048189.
5. Hearne, "Lucid Dreams."

Chapter 15

1. LaBerge, *Exploring the World of Lucid Dreaming*, 30.
2. Daniel Erlacher, Michael Schredl, Tsuneo Watanabe, Jun Yaman, and Florian Gantzert, "The Incidence of Lucid Dreaming within a Japanese University Student Sample," *International Journal of Dream Research* 1, no. 2 (2008): 39–43.

3. Michael Schädel and Daniel Erlacher, "Frequency of Lucid Dreaming in a Representative German Sample," *Perceptual and Motor Skills* 112 (2011): 104–108.

4. Kelly Bulkeley, "Lucid Dreaming by the Numbers," in *Lucid Dreaming: New Perspectives on Consciousness in Sleep*, Vol. 1: Science, Psychology, and Education (Santa Barbara, CA: ABC-CLIO, 2014), 1–22.

5. Bulkeley, "Lucid Dreaming by the Numbers," 9.

6. Walker, *Why We Sleep*, 296.

Chapter 16

1. Gackenbach and Hunt, "Deeper Inquiry," 9.

Chapter 17

1. "Out-of-Body Experience,"*Merriam-Webster*, https://www.merriam-webster.com/dictionary/out-of-body experience.

2. "Astral Projection," *Merriam-Webster*, https://www.merriam-webster.com/dictionary/astral projection.

3. "Astral Projection," *Lexico*, https://www.lexico.com/en/definition/astral_projection.

4. Ursula Voss et al., "Induction of Self Awareness in Dreams through Frontal Low Current Stimulation of Gamma Activity," *Nature Neuroscience* 17, no. 6 (2014), doi:10.1038/nn.3719.

Chapter 18

1. J. Allan Hobson and Edward F. Pace-Schott, "The Cognitive Neuroscience of Sleep: Neuronal Systems, Consciousness and Learning," *Nature Reviews Neuroscience* 3, no. 9 (2002), doi:10.1038/nrn915.

2. Filevich et al., "Metacognitive Mechanisms Underlying Lucid Dreaming."

3. Ursula Voss and A. Hobson, "What Is the State-of-the-Art on Lucid Dreaming? Recent Advances and Questions for Future Research," *Open MIND* (2015), doi:10.15502/9783958570306.

4. Voss and Voss, "Neurobiological Model of Lucid Dreaming," 26–27.

5. Brown, *Dreaming Wide Awake*, 50–51.

6. Wangyal and Dahlby, *Tibetan Yogas of Dream and Sleep*, 146.

7. Timothy Leary, Ralph Metzner, and Richard Alpert, "The Psychedelic Experience," accessed September 13, 2019, http://www.leary.ru/download/leary/Timothy Leary—The Tibetan Book Of The Dead.pdf.

Chapter 19

1. Malcolm Godwin, *The Lucid Dreamer: A Waking Guide for the Traveler between Worlds* (New York: Simon and Schuster, 1994), 25.

2. LaBerge, *Exploring the World of Lucid Dreaming*, 25.

3. Daniel Erlacher, Melanie Schadlich, Tadas Stumbrys, and Michael Schredl, "Time for Actions in Lucid Dreams: Effects of Task Modality, Length, and Complexity," *Frontiers in Psychology* 4 (2014), https://doi.org/10.3389/fpsyg.2013.01013.

4. Wangyal and Dahlby, *Tibetan Yogas of Dream and Sleep*, 20.

5. Ibid., 16.

6. Ibid., 78.

Chapter 20

1. Watson, "To Dream, Perchance to Remember."

2. M. Balgrove and S. J. Hartnell, "Lucid Dreaming: Associations with Internal Locus of Control, Need for Cognition and Creativity," *Personality and Individual Differences* 28, no. 1 (2000), doi:10.1016/s0191-8869(99)00078-1.

3. Voss et al., "Induction of Self Awareness."

Bibliography

"Astral Projection." Lexico. n.d. http://www.lexico.com/en/definition/astral_project ion.

"Astral Projection." *Merriam-Webster.* n.d. http://merriam-webster.com/dictionary/astral projection.

Balgrove, M., and S. J. Hartnell. "Lucid Dreaming: Associations with Internal Locus of Control, Need for Cognition and Creativity." *Personality and Individual Differences* 28, no. 1 (2000): 41–47. doi:10.1016/s0191–8869(99)00078–1.

Bergmann, Peter. "8 Things the Mushroom Told Terence McKenna." McKennite. April 30, 2016. http://www.mckennite.com/articles/voice.

Bolla, Karen I., Suzanne R. Lesage, Charlene E. Gamaldo, David N. Neubauer, Frank R. Funderburk, Jean Lud Cadet, Paula M. David, Antonio Verdejo-Garcia, and Amy R. Benbrook. "Sleep Disturbance in Heavy Marijuana Users." *Sleep* 31, no. 6 (2008): 901–908. https://doi.org/10.1093/sleep/31.6.901.

Boutsikaris, Costa. "Terrence Mckenna 2012 Eternity." YouTube. October 8, 2008. Accessed June 15, 2019. https://www.youtube.com/watch?v=QkSxKGkNs6M.

Brown, David Jay. *Dreaming Wide Awake: Lucid Dreaming, Shamanic Healing, and Psychedelics.* Rochester, VT: Inner Traditions, 2016.

Bulkeley, Kelly. *An Introduction to the Psychology of Dreaming.* 2nd ed. Santa Barbara, CA: Praeger, 2017.

Bulkeley, Kelly. "Lucid Dreaming by the Numbers." In *Lucid Dreaming: New Perspectives on Consciousness in Sleep,* 1–22. Vol. 1: Science, Psychology, and Education. Santa Barbara, CA: ABC-CLIO, 2014.

de Koninck, J., D. Lorrain, G. Christ, G. Proulx, and D. Coulombe. "Intensive Language Learning and Increases in Rapid Eye Movement Sleep: Evidence of a Performance Factor." *International Journal of Psychophysiology* 8, no. 1 (1989): 43–47. doi:10.1016/0167-8760(89)90018-4.

Dement, William, and Nathaniel Kleitman. "The Relation of Eye Movements During Sleep to Dream Activity: An Objective Method for the Study of Dreaming." *Journal of Experimental Psychology* 53, no. 5 (1957): 339–346. doi:10.1037/h0048189.

Erlacher, Daniel, Melanie Schädlich, Tadas Stumbrys, and Michael Schredl. "Time for Actions in Lucid Dreams: Effects of Task Modality, Length, and Complexity." *Frontiers in Psychology* 4 (2014). doi:10.3389/fpsyg.2013.01013.

Erlacher, Daniel, Michael Schredl, Tsuneo Watanabe, Jun Yaman, and Florian Gantzert. "The Incidence of Lucid Dreaming Within a Japanese University Student Sample." *International Journal of Dream Research* 1, no. 2 (2008): 39–43.

Filevich, E., M. Dresler, T. R. Brick, and S. Kuhn. "Metacognitive Mechanisms Underlying Lucid Dreaming." *Journal of Neuroscience* 35, no. 3 (2015): 1082–1088. doi:10.1523/jneurosci.3342–14.2015.

Bibliography

Gackenbach, J., and H. Hunt. "A Deeper Inquiry Into the Association Between Lucid Dreams and Video Game Play." In *Lucid Dreaming: New Perspectives on Consciousness in Sleep,* 9. Vol. 1: Science, Psychology, and Education. Santa Barbara, CA: ABC-CLIO, 2014.

Gackenbach, J., R. Crandon, and C. Alexander. "Lucid Dreaming, Witnessing Dreaming, and the Transcendental Meditation Technique." *Lucidity Letter 5* (1986): 34–40.

Godwin, Malcolm. *The Lucid Dreamer: A Waking Guide for the Traveler between Worlds.* New York: Simon & Schuster, 1994.

Hall, Calvin, and Robert Van de Castle. *The Content Analysis of Dreams.* New York: Appleton-Century-Crofts, 1966.

"Hallucination." (2020). Lexico Dictionaries. https://www.lexico.com/en/definition/hallucination

Hearne, Keith. "Lucid Dreams: An Electrophysiological and Psychological Study." Unpublished PhD thesis, University of Hull, 1978.

Hobson, J. Allan. *Sleep.* New York: Scientific American Library, 1995.

Hobson, J. Allan, and Edward F. Pace-Schott. "The Cognitive Neuroscience of Sleep: Neuronal Systems, Consciousness and Learning." *Nature Reviews Neuroscience* 3, no. 9 (2002): 679–693. doi:10.1038/nrn915.

Holzinger, Brigitte. "Lucid Dreaming in Psychotherapy." In *Lucid Dreaming: New Perspectives on Consciousness in Sleep,* 35–61. Vol. 1: Science, Psychology, and Education. Santa Barbara, CA: ABC-CLIO, 2014.

Irwin, Lee. "Memory, Meaning, and Imagination in Lucid Dreams." In *Lucid Dreaming: New Perspectives on Consciousness in Sleep,* 101–126. Vol 1: Science, Psychology, and Education. Santa Barbara, CA: ABC-CLIO, 2014.

"Jon Kabat-Zinn: Defining Mindfulness." *Mindful.* January 11, 2019. Accessed June 14, 2019. https://www.mindful.org/jon-kabat-zinn-defining-mindfulness/.

LaBerge, S., and H. Rheingold. *Exploring the World of Lucid Dreaming.* New York: Ballantine Books, 2007.

LaBerge, S., Lynne Levitan, & William Dement. "Lucid Dreaming: Physiological Correlates of Consciousness during REM Sleep," *The Journal of Mind and Behavior* 7, no. 2/3 (Spring and Summer, 1986): 251–258

La Marca, and LaBerge. "PreSleep Treatment" poster session. DWA.

Leary, Timothy, Ralph Metzner, and Richard Alpert. "The Psychedelic Experience." http://www.leary.ru/download/leary/Timothy Leary—The Tibetan Book Of The Dead.pdf.

McLuhan, Marshall, and Gordon W. Terrence. *Understanding Media: The Extensions of Man.* Berkeley, CA: Gingko Press, 2015; originally published 1964.

McNamara, P. "The Dream Lag Effect: Dreams Participate in Memory Consolidation." May 15, 2011. Accessed May 20, 2019. https://www.psychologytoday.com/us/blog/dream-catcher/201105/the-dream-lag-effect.

Newmark, T. "Cases in Visualization for Improved Athletic Performance." *Psychiatric Annals,* 34, no. 10 (2012): 385–387. Doi: 10.3928/00485713-20121003-07

Nielsen, T.A., D. L. McGregor, A. Zadra, D. Ilnicki, and L. Oullet. "Pain in Dreams." *Sleep* 16, no. 5 (August 1, 1993). http://doi.org/10.1093/sleep/16.5.490.

O'Brien, F. *The Third Policeman.* London: MacGibbon, 1967.

"Out-of-Body Experience." *Merriam-Webster,* n.d. http://merriam-webster.com/dictionary/out-of-body experience.

Page, James F. "Lucid Dreaming as Sleep Meditation." In *Lucid Dreaming: New Perspectives on Consciousness in Sleep,* 63–76. Vol. 1: Science, Psychology, and Education. Santa Barbara, CA: ABC-CLIO, 2014.

"REM Sleep Behavior Disorder," *Sleep Foundation,* accessed April 8, 2020, https://www.sleepfoundation.org/articles/rem-sleep-behavior-disorder

Bibliography

Schädel, Michael, and D. Erlacher. "Frequency of Lucid Dreaming in a Representative German Sample." *Perceptual and Motor Skills* 112 (2011): 104–108.

Sharpless, B. A., and J. P. Barber. "Lifetime Prevalence Rates of Sleep Paralysis: A Systematic Review." *Sleep Medicine Reviews* 15, no. 5 (2011): 311–315. doi:10.1016/j.smrv.2011.01.007.

Siegel, J.M. "The Evolution of REM Sleep," *Handbook of Behavioral State Control.* Berkeley, CA: Gingko Press, 2015; originally published 1964.

Voss, Ursula, and A. Hobson. "What Is the State-of-the-Art on Lucid Dreaming? Recent Advances and Questions for Future Research." *Open MIND* (2015). doi:10.15502/9783958570306.

Voss, Ursula, and Georg Voss. "A Neurobiological Model of Lucid Dreaming." In *Lucid Dreaming: New Perspectives on Consciousness in Sleep,* 23–36. Vol. 1: Science, Psychology, and Education. Santa Barbara, CA: ABC-CLIO, 2014.

Voss, Ursula, Romain Holzmann, Allan Hobson, Walter Paulus, Judith Koppehele-Gossel, Ansgar Klimke, and Michael A. Nitsche. "Induction of Self Awareness in Dreams Through Frontal Low Current Stimulation of Gamma Activity." *Nature Neuroscience* 17, no. 6 (2014): 810–812. doi:10.1038/nn.3719.

Waggoner, R. *Lucid Dreaming: Gateway to the Inner Self.* Needham, MA: Moment Point Press, 2008.

Walker, Matthew P. *Why We Sleep: Unlocking the Power of Sleep and Dreams.* New York: Scribner's, 2017.

Wangyal, Tenzin. *The Tibetan Yogas of Dream and Sleep.* Ithaca, NY: Snow Lion Publications, 1998.

Watson, David. "To Dream, Perchance to Remember: Individual Differences in Dream Recall." *Personality and Individual Differences* 34, no. 7 (2003): 1271–1286.

Index

Index